IMPLEMENTING
Integrated Performance
Assessment

Bonnie Adair-Hauck
University of Pittsburgh

Eileen W. Glisan
Indiana University of Pennsylvania

Francis J. Troyan
The Ohio State University

ACTFL AMERICAN COUNCIL ON THE
TEACHING OF FOREIGN LANGUAGES

The American Council on the Teaching of Foreign Languages
1001 North Fairfax Street, Suite 200
Alexandria, VA 22314

Graphic Design by Paintbox Creative, LLC
Edited by Marty Abbott, Executive Director, and Paul Sandrock, Director of Education

Second printing 2015
© 2013 by The American Council on the Teaching of Foreign Languages, Alexandria, VA

ISBN: 978-0-9705798-6-7

What's New in the Second Edition of the Integrated Performance Assessment Manual?

The second edition of the IPA Manual builds upon the original framework presented to guide instructors in designing and implementing this cutting-edge assessment into their language classrooms. As in the first edition, the revised manual presents an in-depth rationale for using the IPA; describes the IPA construct in detail, in particular the unique features that sets it apart from other assessments; outlines step-by-step procedures for implementing the IPA and for connecting it to instruction in a seamless manner; and introduces scoring rubrics that can be used for assessing performance in the tasks across the three modes of communication.

Since its inception in 1997, the IPA has been embraced by instructors at various levels of instruction as well as by foreign language education researchers. The interest in the IPA has grown from the initial pilot group of teachers in 1999 to its current use in elementary, secondary and post-secondary settings as well as in several states as a state-level assessment (see Chapter 7). Given the current expanded scope of the IPA, the impetus for producing a second edition of the manual arose from a need to disseminate a) findings from research conducted on the IPA since 2003; b) expanded guidelines for how to design and implement the IPA as well as how to provide feedback and modeling; c) a set of model IPAs created by instructors who have implemented the assessment over the past decade; d) revised rubrics that can be used more effectively to rate learner performance across the three modes of communication; and e) ways in which the IPA has had an impact on teacher perceptions, classroom instruction, and learning.

The reader will find the following *new* elements in the second edition:

1. A description of the research that has been conducted on the IPA together with findings that shed light on student performance across the three modes of communication and the impact of the IPA on instruction (Chapter 3)

2. Presentation of the IPA as a tool for backward planning (Chapters 1 and 4)

3. A re-conceptualized rubric for the interpretive mode, and the use of a single interpretive rubric across IPA levels (Chapter 2)

4. The addition of Interpersonal and Presentational rubrics for the Advanced level, particularly for use at the post-secondary level (Chapter 2)

5. A newly developed discussion of modeling and the features of a co-constructive approach to IPA feedback, with samples of discourse of co-constructive feedback sessions for the Interpersonal mode (Chapter 5)

6. Model IPAs in Arabic, Chinese, French, Latin, and Spanish, at the Novice, Intermediate, Intermediate High, and Advanced levels (Chapter 6)

7. Details regarding how to use the IPA rubrics to provide feedback and grades to students (Chapter 2)

8. A description of the impact that the IPA has had on teacher perceptions, classroom instruction, and learning (Chapter 7)

The following elements of the first edition have been significantly *expanded*:

1. Rationale for the IPA in terms of current educational endeavors and frameworks (Chapter 1)

2. Guidelines for how to design and implement IPAs (Chapter 2)

3. Strategies for preparing learners for the IPA across the three modes of communication; linking instruction and the IPA (Chapter 4)

4. Factors to consider when selecting authentic texts for the Interpretive Tasks (Chapter 4)

5. Sample authentic texts (Chapters 4, 6, and Appendices)

6. Interpersonal and Presentational IPA Rubrics (Appendices)

7. IPA Glossary of Terms (Glossary)

8. IPA References (List of References included at end of each chapter)

This manual has been designed for educators at any level who are interested in implementing the IPA. In-service teachers might use this manual for purposes of professional development, particularly along with an IPA workshop. In addition, methods instructors can use it to introduce the IPA to their K-12 foreign language teacher candidates and/or post-secondary teaching assistants. The manual might also be used by faculty who wish to use the IPA as a tool for planning curriculum and/or for establishing the IPA as a district- or state-wide assessment. Researchers will find many ideas in the IPA manual for conducting further research on the assessment. Undoubtedly this manual will be a valuable resource to all foreign language educators who are in search of a cutting-edge strategy for blending instruction and assessment in a seamless fashion.

Acknowledgements

We would like to thank the American Council on the Teaching of Foreign Languages, under the leadership of Marty Abbott, Executive Director, for supporting our work on the IPA and for funding the second edition of this manual. We are deeply indebted to the original Standards Assessment Design Project Task Force, who designed the IPA:

Elvira Swender, ACTFL, Project Director
S. Paul Sandrock, ACTFL (formerly Wisconsin Department of Instruction), Project Coodinator
Bonnie Adair-Hauck, University of Pittsburgh (PA)
Eileen W. Glisan, Indiana University of Pennsylvania
Keiko Koda, Carnegie Mellon University, Pittsburgh, PA
Michael Stewart, Standard & Poors, New York, NY

We acknowledge the early contributions of Everett Kline of the Center on Learning, Assessment, and School Structure [CLASS] (Pennington, NJ), and Greg Duncan, InterPrep, Inc., Marietta, GA, who helped shape the original IPA design.

The following individuals played a pivotal role in the field testing of the early versions of the IPA:

Pilot Site Coordinators
Martha G. Abbott, Fairfax County Public Schools, VA
Peggy Boyles, Putnam City Schools, OK
Donna Clementi, Appleton West High School, WI
Deborah Lindsay, Greater Albany School District, OR
Frank Mulhern, Wallingford-Swarthmore School District, PA
Kathleen Riordan, Springfield Public Schools, MA

Teachers/Assessment Fellows at Pilot Sites
Rosa Alvaro-Alves, Springfield Public Schools, MA
Linda Bahr, Greater Albany School District, OR
Carolyn Carroll, Fairfax County Public Schools, VA
Christine Carroll, Putnam City Schools, OK
Kathy Ceman, Butte des Morts Elementary, WI
Donna Clementi, Appleton West High School, WI
Karin Cochran, Jesuit High School, OR
Michele de Cruz-Sainz, Wallingford-Swarthmore School District, PA
Margaret Draheim, Appleton East High School, WI
Cathy Etheridge, Appleton East High School, WI
Carmen Felix-Fournier, Springfield Public Schools, MA
Catherine Field, Greater Albany School District, OR
Stephen Flesher, Beaverton Public Schools, OR
Nancy Gadbois, Springfield Public Schools, MA
Frederic Gautzsch, Wallingford-Swarthmore School District, PA
Susana Gorski, Nicolet Elementary School, WI
Susan Harding, Putnam City Schools, OK
Heidi Helmich, Madison Middle School, WI
Mei-Ju Hwang, Springfield Public Schools, MA

Betty Ivich, Putnam City Schools, OK
Michael Kraus, Putnam City Schools, OK
Irmgard Langacker, Wallingford-Swarthmore School District, PA
Dorothy Lavigne, Wallingford-Swarthmore School District, PA
Deborah Lindsay, Greater Albany School District, PA
Conrad Lower, Wallingford-Swarthmore School District, PA
Linda S. Meyer, Appleton North High School, WI
Paula J. Meyer, Appleton North High School, WI
Linda Moore, Putnam City Schools, OK
Frank Mulhern, Wallingford-Swarthmore School District, PA
Rita Oleksak, Springfield Public Schools, MA
Frances Pettigrew, Fairfax County Public Schools, VA
Rebecca Rowton, Rollingwood Elementary School, OK
Ann Smith, Jesuit High School, OR
Dee Dee Stafford, Putnam City Schools, OK
Adam Stryker, Fairfax County Public Schools, VA
Catherine Thurber, Tigard High School, OR
Ghislaine Tulou, Fairfax County Public Schools, VA
Carter Vaden, Fairfax County Public Schools, VA
Sally Ziebell, Putnam City Schools, OK

Students of:
Albany High School, Albany, OR
Appleton Area Public Schools, WI
Beaverton Public Schools, OR
Fairfax County Public Schools, VA
Putnam City Public Schools, OK
Public Schools of Springfield, MA
Wallington-Swarthmore Schools, PA

This second edition would not have been possible without the contributions of the following individuals:

Myriam Abdel-Malek, University of Pittsburgh
Tara Aucoin, Mahwah Public Schools, New Jersey
Ruta Couet, South Carolina Department of Education
Ashlie Hellman, Falk School, University of Pittsburgh
Jay McTighe, Jay McTighe and Assoicates
Mandy Menke, Grand Valley State University
José Pan, Edison School District
Michele J. Schreiner, Egg harbor Township Public Schools
Tracey Seiler, South Carolina Virtual School Program
Paula Staile-Costa, College of New Jersey
Grant Wiggins, Authentic Education, Hopewell New Jersey
Daniel Uribe, US Air Force Academy

Students of:
Casco Bay High School, Portland, Maine

We are grateful to Richard Donato, University of Pittsburgh, for his assistance in helping us to re-conceptualize the Interpretive mode in the IPA re-design.

Table of Contents

Chapter 1

Rationale: Why the Need for Integrated Performance Assessment?

For well over two decades, the field of language education has placed increasing emphasis on the need to prepare our U.S. citizenry with the linguistic skills and cultural understanding necessary to interact with diverse groups of people who speak languages other than English. This goal has driven the development of several national initiatives resulting in a new paradigm for planning and teaching that focuses on language learners: what they should know and be able to do with the language and how they should be actively engaged in learning and constructing meaning in real-world contexts beyond the classroom setting (Shrum & Glisan, 2010).

The national *Standards for Foreign Language Learning in the 21st Century* (National Standards in Foreign Language Education Project [NSFLEP]), first released in 1996 and expanded in 1999 and 2006, provide a vision for language learning based on assumptions regarding the role of linguistic and cultural competence in the global community, the circumstances under which learners can be successful in acquiring this competence, and the place of language and culture education within the core curriculum (NSFLEP, 2006). To this end, the Standards offer:

- A vision for the future of language and culture education;

- A rationale for the inclusion of all students in language study;

- Realistic expectations for student performance over an extended sequence of language study and at benchmark points (grades 4, 8, 12, 16);

- A framework for development of state and local standards; and

- Innovative ways of implementing instructional resources.

The Standards feature five Goal Areas, known as the "Five Cs of Foreign Language Education," which provide a rationale for language education: Communication, Cultures, Connections, Comparisons, and Communities. Each goal area delineates two to three content standards that describe the knowledge and skills that learners should demonstrate as a result of their language study (See www.actfl.org to access the Standards). The Standards re-conceptualized several traditional aspects of language study in terms of:

1. Broadening of the definition of the content of the language curriculum to include not only the language system and cultural knowledge but also content from other subject areas, critical thinking skills, learning strategies, communication strategies, and technology.

2. The depiction of "communication" in terms of three modes—interpersonal, interpretive, presentational—that place primary emphasis on the context and purpose of meaningful communication.

3. An anthropological view of "culture" based on the relationship between and among cultural products, cultural practices, and cultural perspectives or attitudes and values (NSFLEP, 2006).

With the development of the National Standards came a call for an assessment that could be used to assess learners' progress in meeting the standards across the five goal areas.

The concern about assessing the functional speaking ability of students who complete second language programs goes back to the late 1970s, when U.S. President Jimmy Carter's Commission on Foreign Language and International Studies recommended that the profession develop language proficiency tests (*Strength Through Wisdom*, 1979). As a result of an international project to adapt the proficiency scale and oral interview procedure developed earlier by the Foreign Service Institute (FSI) of the U.S. Department of State, the *ACTFL Provisional Proficiency Guidelines* were first published in 1982, together with the ACTFL Oral Proficiency Interview (OPI) (Liskin-Gasparro, 1984). The Guidelines describe what language users are able to do with the language in speaking, writing, listening, and reading at levels of performance labeled Novice, Intermediate, Advanced, and

Superior, with Distinguished added in 2012, as measured against the abilities of an educated native speaker of the language. The Proficiency Guidelines and OPI heralded a shift in instructional focus from "what" was taught (i.e., the contents of a textbook) to what outcomes learners could accomplish as assessed through the OPI and proficiency-based assessments. Since the 1980s, the Proficiency Guidelines, recently released in expanded and revised form, have continued to have a pivotal impact on instruction and assessment (ACTFL, 2012c; Liskin-Gasparro, 2003). Further, current research in the field is pointing to the importance of longitudinal assessment to track the development of proficiency over time in extended sequences of language instruction (Donato & Tucker, 2010). See Appendix A for the major levels of the ACTFL Rating Scale as depicted in the inverted pyramid and Appendix B for an overview of the assessment criteria used to assess proficiency in speaking.

While the *ACTFL Proficiency Guidelines* continue to describe language proficiency in the four skills, their connection to the Communication goal area of the national Standards is obvious. However, to delineate the specific performance of language learners at various K-12 benchmarks of learning and development, ACTFL published its *ACTFL Performance Guidelines for K-12 Learners* in 1998 and recently revised and renamed them the *ACTFL Performance Descriptors for Language Learners* (2012b). The Performance Descriptors describe how well language learners perform in an instructional setting at various points along the language learning continuum from Novice to Intermediate to Advanced ranges of performance. These descriptors define performance outcomes in terms of language functions, contexts/content, text types, language control, vocabulary use, communication strategies, and cultural awareness.

The majority of states and local districts have aligned their curricula with the Standards to continue the impetus toward teaching for real world competence in the goal areas of Communication, Cultures, Connections, Comparisons, and Communities. In addition, an increasing number of post-secondary language programs are revising their curricula to reflect standards-based outcomes. The *ACTFL Proficiency Guidelines* have provided the field with a com-

mon yardstick for assessing functional proficiency in real-world situations in spontaneous and non-rehearsed contexts (ACTFL, 2012c), while the *ACTFL Performance Descriptors for Language Learners* provide a roadmap for teaching and learning and assist teachers in setting expectations at the summative assessment level. What had heretofore been missing for instructors, however, was a valid way of measuring student progress toward standards within a proficiency-based instructional context. The Integrated Performance Assessment (IPA) provides a means for answering questions that K-16 instructors are asking, such as:

Am I assessing performance using real-world tasks that are meaningful to students?

Am I assessing in the same way that students are learning in my classroom?

How can I more effectively assess the abilities of my students in the three modes of communication as they relate to the ACTFL Performance Descriptors for Language Learners?

Are my students making progress toward the Intermediate or Advanced proficiency levels as defined in the ACTFL Proficiency Guidelines?

How can I develop and manage classroom discourse so that it reflects the spirit of interpersonal communication and the characteristics of conversation that occurs in the world beyond the classroom?

What kind of feedback will improve student performance?

Are my students becoming the kind of independent, life-long language learners that they will need to be to improve and maintain their language skills to meet the demands of the 21st Century?

The ACTFL IPA was designed to address the national need for assessing learner progress in meeting the content areas of the National Standards, in demonstrating performance depicted in the *ACTFL Performance Descriptors*, and in illustrating progress toward specific proficiency levels in the *ACTFL Proficiency Guidelines*. Taking into account the interconnected nature of communication, the IPA enables learners to demonstrate their ability to communicate within specific goal areas of the National Standards across the interpersonal, interpretive, and presentational modes of communication. In short, the IPA has filled the previously existing void for an assessment that could determine the level at which learners interpret authentic texts in the foreign language, interact with others using the target language in oral and written form, and present oral and printed messages to audiences of listeners and readers. The IPA prototype outlines a process for going beyond current practice in language testing.

Analyzed through the lens of the broader educational field beyond language teaching, the IPA builds upon current research on assessment and approaches to instructional planning. According to Wiggins (1998), *educative* tests (i.e., those that improve the performance of both learner and teacher) must feature *authentic* tasks, or those that mirror the tasks and challenges encountered by individuals in the real world. An assessment task, such as those featured in the IPA, is authentic if it:

- is realistic in that it tests the learner's knowledge and abilities in real-world situations;

- requires judgment and innovation;

- asks the student to "do" the [academic] subject rather than reciting information so that the student carries out a task using the language in a meaningful way;

- replicates or simulates the contexts in which adults are "tested" in the workplace, in civic life, and in personal life so that students address an actual audience, not just their teacher;

- assesses the student's ability to use a repertoire of knowledge and skill efficiently and effectively to negotiate a complex task; and

- allows appropriate opportunities to rehearse, practice, consult resources, and get feedback, and refine performances and products (Wiggins & McTighe, 2005, p. 154).

In recent years, the key role of assessment in improving learner performance and informing instruction has been acknowledged. In this vein, Wiggins (1993) traced the word

assessment to its Latin root *assidere*, meaning "to sit with," and he contends that assessment is something we should do *with* students rather than *to* them (as cited in Phillips, 2006, p. 83). Indeed current research calls for assessment practices whose primary purpose is to inform teaching and learning (Bachman, 2007; Poehner & Lantolf, 2003; McNamara, 2001; Wiggins, 1998; Wiggins & McTighe, 2005). Further, this novel conceptualization of assessment is now international in scope as language researchers in countries such as Australia, Canada, Colombia, England, Hong Kong, Israel, and Taiwan are suggesting assessment instruments that form an *assessment bridge* (Colby-Kelly's term, 2007) between teaching and learning (Black, Harrison, Lee, Marshall, & William, 2003; Gardner, 2006; Leung, 2004; Muñoz & Alvarez, 2010).

As will be explored in detail later in this manual, the IPA is predicated on a "backward design" approach in which learners understand the criteria and standards for the tasks they are striving to master before they are asked to perform. This model features a "cyclical approach" to second language learning and development, in which learners perform, practice, and receive feedback before, during, and after the IPA. Figure 1.1 illustrates the three stages of backward design, in which the teacher first identifies the desired end results of instruction, then determines the evidence that will verify that the end results have been achieved, and finally plans learning experiences that will enable learners to demonstrate the end results (Wiggins & McTighe, 2005). What is striking about this type of approach is that 1) it combines instruction and assessment in a seamless manner and 2) it contrasts sharply with the traditional approach of planning instructional activities (i.e., often from a textbook) *first* and designing assessments *later* in the instructional process. According to Wiggins and McTighe (2005), educators who use backward design think first like assessors, then like curriculum designers, and finally like activity designers. The advantage of the IPA within a backward design approach is that the target for performance is always in focus, and consequently both learners and instructors understand what the goal is and how instruction and assessment work as one system to enable learners to reach that goal.

Figure 1.1 Stages of Backward Design

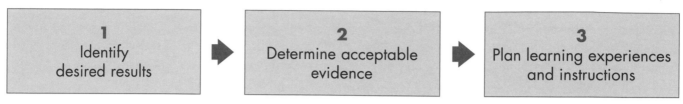

Source: Wiggins & McTighe, 2005, p. 18.

While being situated within current research-based approaches to assessment and instructional planning, the IPA reflects principles of brain-based research for student learning and Bloom's Taxonomy of Thinking (Bloom, Engelhart, Furst, Hill, & Krathwohl, 1956). The findings of brain-based research applied to learning a second language illustrate that the brain stores information based on functionality and meaningfulness, that rehearsal is necessary for retention, and that practice alone doesn't "make perfect" unless the learner has received feedback indicating what needs to be done to improve (Kennedy, 2006; Sousa, 2006). The IPA addresses these findings by featuring authentic tasks that are meaningful and by promoting the cycle of practice, performance, and feedback. Further, it promotes higher-order thinking processes as depicted in Bloom's Taxonomy (Anderson & Krathwohl, 2001; Bloom, et al., 1956), which depicts six levels of complexity of human thought. While Bloom's Taxonomy has been used for over fifty years in education to help teachers understand the level of thinking required by their classroom objectives and activities, it has played a pivotal role in assisting teachers in moving their students to higher levels of thinking. The tasks of the IPA are sequenced to move students through the taxonomy by guiding them from understanding an authentic text to applying their newly acquired knowledge in an oral interpersonal task to creating a presentation for an audience of readers or listeners.

In addition to answering the call made by researchers both at home and abroad for a standards-based assessment that measures proficiency, the IPA also conceptualizes foreign language as operating in concert with other disciplines and 21st century skills. The Partnership for 21st Century Skills

(2011a) recently developed a collective vision of learning known as the "Framework for 21st Century Learning," which combines a focus on 21st century student outcomes with "innovative support systems" to assist students in acquiring the abilities required in the 21st century (See Appendix C). The Partnership (P21) has made alliances with national organizations that represent the core academic subjects, which have resulted in the creation of 21st Century Skills Maps that depict the intersection between the core subject areas and 21st Century Skills. In 2011, ACTFL released its P21 World Languages Skills Map, which illustrates the relationship between language learning and the various 21st century skill areas. The IPA prepares language learners for the challenges of life and work in the 21st century by providing them with opportunities to develop:

- visual and information literacy
- cultural literacy and global awareness
- curiosity, creativity and risk-taking
- higher-order thinking and sound reasoning
- teaming and collaboration
- interactive communication
- effective use of real-world tools
- life and career skills (Partnership for 21st Century Skills, 2011b).

In this role as a key component in an innovative support system for learning in the 21st century, the IPA and its co-constructive approach to feedback on performance (Adair-Hauck & Troyan, 2013; See Chapter 5 for a discussion) holds potential to shift students' learning mindset. The psychological research on mindset by Dweck and her colleagues (e.g., Blackwell, Trzesniewski, & Dweck, 2007; Dweck, 2006, 2007) identified two mindsets: the fixed mindset and the growth mindset. In the fixed mindset, the student views his or her intelligence as unchangeable. This type of student seeks to "look smart at all costs" (Dweck, 2007, p. 7). By contrast, students with a growth mindset perceive challenges as opportunities to learn by working hard to face and overcome their weaknesses. The IPA is an assessment system that can promote a growth mindset in student language performance through meaningful co-constructed feedback.

Finally, the IPA is aligned with new *Common Core State Standards for English Language Arts and Literacy in History/Social Studies, Science, and Technical Subjects* [henceforth referred to as the "Common Core State Standards" (CCSS)] (National Governors Association Center for Best Practices, Council of Chief State School Officers [CCSSO], 2010). The CCSS promote an integrated approach to instruction that develops communicative skills across a variety of spoken and written text types (CCSSO, 2010, p. 5). In 2012, ACTFL linked the three modes of communication of the National Standards (interpersonal, interpretive and presentational) and the Common Core State Standards to clearly focus foreign language instruction on "the purpose behind the communication" (ACTFL, 2012a, p. 1). This connecting of the National Standards and the Common Core State Standards situates the IPA as a key assessment instrument in the era of the Common Core State Standards (Troyan, 2013).

In sum, the Integrated Performance Assessment has filled the need for a tool that assesses learners' progress in meeting the National Standards and attaining proficiency levels on the continuum of the *ACTFL Proficiency Guidelines*. Further, it fits well within current research-based educational paradigms that stress the importance of higher-order thinking skills and feedback for improving learner performance. Finally, it represents a visionary approach for integrating teaching, learning, and assessment in a seamless fashion so that these elements work in concert to impact classroom learning.

References

Adair-Hauck, B., & Troyan, F.J. (2013). A descriptive and co-constructive approach to Integrated Performance Assessment feedback. *Foreign Language Annals, 46*, 23-44.

American Council on the Teaching of Foreign Languages (ACTFL). (1982). *ACTFL provisional proficiency guidelines.* Hastings-on-Hudson, NY: Author.

American Council on the Teaching of Foreign Languages (ACTFL). (1998). *ACTFL performance guidelines for K–12 learners.* Yonkers, NY: Author.

American Council on the Teaching of Foreign Languages (ACTFL). (1999). *ACTFL proficiency guidelines—Speaking.* Yonkers, NY: Author.

American Council on the Teaching of Foreign Languages (ACTFL). (2001). *ACTFL proficiency guidelines—Writing.* Yonkers, NY: Author.

American Council on the Teaching of Foreign Languages (ACTFL). (2012a). *Alignment of the National Standards for Learning Languages with the Common Core State Standards.* Alexandria, VA: Author. Retrieved from http://www.actfl.org/sites/default/files/pdfs/Aligning_CCSS_Language_Standards_v6.pdf

American Council on the Teaching of Foreign Languages (ACTFL). (2012b). *ACTFL performance descriptors for language learners.* Alexandria, VA: Author.

American Council on the Teaching of Foreign Languages (ACTFL). (2012c). *ACTFL Proficiency Guidelines-Speaking, Writing, Listening and Reading,* 3rd ed. Alexandria, VA: Author.

Anderson, L. W., & Krathwohl, D. R. (Eds.). (2001). *A taxonomy for learning, teaching and assessing: A revision of Bloom's Taxonomy of educational objectives.* New York : Longman.

Bachman, L. F. (2007). What is the construct? The dialectic of abilities and contexts in defining constructs in language assessment. In J. Fox, M. Wesche, & D. Bayliss (Eds.), *What are we measuring? Language testing reconsidered* (pp. 41-71). Ottawa: University of Ottawa Press.

Black, P., Harrison, C., Lee, C., Marshall, B., & Wiliam, D. (2003). *Assessment for learning: Putting it into practice.* Berkshire, England: McGraw-Hill Education.

Blackwell, L. S., Trzesniewski, K. H., & Dweck, C. S. (2007). Implicit theories of intelligence predict achievement across an adolescent transition: A longitudinal study and an intervention. *Child Development, 78,* 246-263.

Bloom, B.-S. (Ed.), Engelhart, M. C., Furst, E. J., Hill, W. H., & Krathwohl, D. R., (1956). *Taxonomy of educational objectives: The classification of educational goals, by a committee of college and university examiners. Handbook 1: Cognitive domain.* New York: Longman.

Colby-Kelly, C., & Turner, C. E. (2007). AFL Research in the L2 classroom and evidence of usefulness: Taking formative assessment to the next level. *The Canadian Modern Language Review, 64,* 9-37.

Donato, R., & Tucker, G. R. (2010). A tale of two schools: Developing sustainable early foreign language programs. Bristol: Multilingual Matters.

Dweck, C. S. (2006). *Mindset: The new psychology of success.* New York: Random House.

Dweck, C. S. (2007). Boosting achievement with messages that motivate. *Education Canada, 47*(2), 6-10.

Gardner, J. (Ed.). (2006). *Assessment and learning.* London: Sage.

Kennedy, T. J. (2006). Language learning and its impact on the brain: Connecting language learning through the mind through content-based instruction. *Foreign Language Annals, 39,* 471-486.

Leung, C. (2004). Developing formative teacher assessment: Knowledge, Practice, and Change. *Language Assessment Quarterly, 1,* 19-41.

Liskin-Gasparro, J. E. (1984). The ACTFL Proficiency Guidelines: A historical perspective. In T. V. Higgs (Ed.), *Teaching for proficiency: The organizing principle.* The ACTFL Foreign Language Education Series (pp. 11–42). Lincolnwood, IL: NTC/Contemporary Publishing Group.

Liskin-Gasparro, J. E. (2003). The ACTFL Proficiency Guidelines and the Oral Proficiency Interview: A brief history and analysis of their survival. *Foreign Language Annals, 36,* 483-490.

McNamara, T. (2001). Language assessment as social practice: Challenges for research. *Language Testing, 18,* 334–399.

Muñoz, A. P., & Álvarez, M. E. (2010). Washback of an oral assessment system in the EFL classroom. *Language Testing, 27*(1), 33-49.

National Governors Association Center for Best Practices, Council of Chief State School Officers (CCSSO). (2010). *Common Core State Standards for English Language Arts and Literacy in History/Social Studies, Science, and Technical Subjects.* (2010). Washington, DC: Author.

National Standards in Foreign Language Education Project (NSFLEP). (1996). *Standards for foreign language learning: Preparing for the 21st century (SFLL).* Lawrence, KS: Allen Press.

National Standards in Foreign Language Education Project (NSFLEP). (1999). *Standards for foreign language learning in the 21st century (SFLL).* Lawrence, KS: Allen Press.

National Standards in Foreign Language Education Project (NSFLEP). (2006). *Standards for foreign language learning in the 21st century (SFLL).* Lawrence, KS: Allen Press.

Partnership for 21st Century Skills. (2011a). *Framework for 21st Century Learning.* Washington, DC. Retrieved from http://www.p21.org/overview.

Partnership for 21st Century Skills. (2011b). *ACTFL P21World Languages Skills Map.* Washington, DC. Retrieved from *http://www.actfl.org/files/21stCenturySkillsMap/p21_worldlanguagesmap.pdf.*

Phillips, J. K. (2006). Assessment now and into the future. In A. L. Heining-Boynton (Ed), *2005-2015: Realizing our vision of languages for all* (pp. 75-103). Upper Saddle River, NJ: Pearson Education, Inc.

Poehner, M. E., & Lantolf, J. P. (2003). *Dynamic assessment of L2 development: Bringing the past into the future.* CALPER Working Papers Series, No. 1. The Pennsylvania State University, Center for Advanced Language Proficiency, Education and Research.

Shrum, J. L., & Glisan, E. W. (2010). *Teacher's handbook: Contextualized language instruction. 4th ed.* Boston, MA: Heinle Cengage Learning.

Sousa, D. A. (2006). *How the brain learns.* Thousand Oaks, CA: Corwin Press.

Strength through wisdom: A critique of U.S. capability. (1979). A report to the President from the President's Commission on Foreign Languages and International Studies. Washington, DC: U.S. Government Printing Office.

Swender, E., & Vicars, R. (2012). *ACTFL oral proficiency interview tester training manual.* Alexandria, VA: American Council on the Teaching of Foreign Languages.

Troyan, F. J. (2013). *Investigating a genre-based approach to writing in an elementary Spanish program.* Unpublished doctoral dissertation. University of Pittsburgh.

Wiggins, G. (1993). *Assessing student performance.* San Francisco: Jossey-Bass.

Wiggins, G. (1998). *Educative assessment.* San Francisco: Jossey-Bass.

Wiggins, G., & McTighe, J. (2005). *Understanding by design.* Alexandria, VA: Association for Supervision and Curriculum Development.

Chapter 2

Description and Design Features of Integrated Performance Assessment

Structure of the IPA

Taking into account the interconnectedness of communication, the Integrated Performance Assessment (IPA) prototype is a multi-task or cluster assessment featuring three tasks, each of which reflects one of the three modes of communication— **interpersonal, interpretive,** and **presentational**—as outlined in the *Standards for Foreign Language Learning in the 21st Century* (National Standards for Foreign Language Education Project, 1996, 1999, 2006).

Interpersonal. The active negotiation of meaning among individuals. Participants observe and monitor one another to see how their intentions and meanings are being communicated. Adjustments and clarifications can be made accordingly. Participants need to initiate, maintain, and at some levels sustain the conversation.

Interpretive. The appropriate interpretation of meanings, including cultural, that occur in written and spoken form (read, heard, or viewed) where there is no recourse to the active negotiation of meaning with the writer or speaker.

Presentational. The creation of oral and written messages in a manner that facilitates interpretation by an audience of listeners, readers, or viewers where no direct opportunity for the active negotiation of meaning exists.

Each task provides the information and elicits the linguistic interaction that is necessary for students to complete the subsequent task. The tasks thus are interrelated and build upon one another. All three tasks are aligned within a single overarching theme or content area (e.g., *Famous Persons, Vacationing in a Hispanic Country*, *Safeguarding the Envi-*

ronment, Crossing Borders, etc.,) that should be of interest to learners and complements the curriculum (see Chapter 4 for discussion of linking assessment and learning through IPA assessment). In keeping with the Standards, IPAs use authentic documents—texts created by native speakers for native speakers (Galloway, 1992) for the interpretive phase of the IPA. By using authentic documents, the Cultures goal area can be seamlessly interwoven into the fabric of an IPA. Depending on the theme and task design for the different modes, IPAs should connect with at least one other goal area: Cultures, Connections, Comparisons, or Communities.

This multi-task or integrative assessment approach reflects the manner in which students naturally acquire and use language in the real world or in the classroom (Glisan, Adair-Hauck, Koda, Sandrock, & Swender, 2003). In real life, listening and reading are oftentimes catalysts for speaking and writing; therefore we recommend starting the IPA with the Interpretive Task. Using the theme of "*Traveling to a Hispanic Country,*" before students can talk or write about a Hispanic country, they would need to read an article about a particular Hispanic country, or listen/watch an advertisement promoting a Hispanic country, view a film etc. In other words, the Interpretive Mode affords learners the opportunity to gain critical content or knowledge of the theme. After the Interpretive Mode, learners have some content with which to interact interpersonally (e.g., discussing pro/cons of visiting a particular Hispanic country or sending email messages to a keypal partner to inquire about a Hispanic country). Finally, the Presentational Mode enables learners to share their thoughts and ideas through presentational speaking or writing (e.g., designing a public service announcement about recycling; creating a brochure to entice students to travel to a Hispanic country). By incorporating the three modes of communication, the IPA is a multi-dimensional, cyclical and integrative assessment. Figure 2.1 captures the cyclical nature and the framework of the Integrated Performance Assessment.

The IPA are designed for learners at four levels of proficiency, which align with the *ACTFL Proficiency Guidelines* (2012c) and the three major ranges of the *ACTFL Performance Descriptors for Language Learners* (2012b): Novice, Intermediate, Intermediate High, and Advanced. It is important to note that in the first edition of this manual, the IPA featured Novice, Intermediate, and Pre-Advanced levels. The term "Pre-Advanced" aligned with Intermediate High of the Proficiency Guidelines, since at the Intermediate High level, users can demonstrate the language functions of the Advanced level, but cannot sustain them in all contexts. This is reflected in the ACTFL Performance Descriptors for Language Learners, and so to avoid confusion, this level is now called "Intermediate High" on the IPA. Four levels of IPAs are presented to offer instructors a tool for capturing the range of performance that is likely to occur in K-16 instructional settings.

Overview of the Tasks

Each IPA begins with a general introduction or overview that describes for the student the context and purpose of the series of authentic tasks. This introduction provides a framework for the assessment and illustrates how each task is integrated into the next and leads up to the culminating task, which results in an oral or written presentational product. The overview may also be shared at the beginning of the instructional sequence (i.e., the unit, semester, or year) leading to the IPA. Moreover, the overview, when presented at the beginning of the instructional sequence, can be paired with exemplars of student performance from previous years, providing an essential model for students (see Chapter 5 for an example and further discussion on modeling). The following is an overview of an Intermediate-level IPA designed by Troyan (2008) titled: "Why Do People Cross Borders?"

Figure 2.1 Integrated Performance Assessment: A Cyclical Approach

I. Interpretive Communication Phase
Students listen to or read an authentic text (e.g., newspaper article, radio broadcast, etc.) and answer information as well as interpretive questions to assess comprehension. (T) provides ss with feedback on performance.

III. Presentational Communication Phase
Students engage in presentational communication by sharing their research/ideas/options. Sample presentational formats: speeches, drama skits, radio broadcasts, posters, brochures, essays, websites, etc.

II. Interpersonal Communication Phase
After receiving feedback regarding Interpretive Phase, ss engaged in interpersonal oral communication about a particular topic which relates to the interpretive text. This phase should be either audio- or videotaped.

Source: Glisan, Adair-Hauck, Koda, Sandrock, and Swender, 2003, p.18.

Overview of Tasks
Intermediate Level
"Why Do People Cross Borders?"
You are studying immigration in your community and beyond. This study has sparked your curiosity to learn as much as possible about the immigration experience. First, you will read about how the province of Québec welcomes newcomers and introduces them to the "fundamentals" of Québec society. Then, based on what you have found out already about immigration, you and a classmate explore ways that newcomers might have difficulty on their arrival. Finally, you will create a storybook about that newcomer's experience and read the book to students at a local French Immersion School.

Note the reason the authors have selected to highlight this IPA in French is because this particular IPA and its impact on teaching and learning have been thoroughly investigated with both quantitative and qualitative data (Adair-Hauck and Troyan, 2013). IPAs in various other languages appear in Chapter 6.

The Interpretive Tasks
The interpretive mode involves activities such as listening to a broadcast or radio commercials; reading an article in a magazine, a short story, or a letter; or viewing a film or video segment. This mode involves not only *literal comprehension* of a text but also *interpretation*, which includes making inferences ("reading between the lines"), identifying cultural perspectives, and offering personal opinions and points of view (Shrum & Glisan, 2010). In each IPA, students read, listen to, or view an authentic text related to the theme of the IPA. It should be noted that in the first edition of this manual, the interpretive mode was treated in a similar manner to that of the interpersonal and presentational modes, inasmuch as tasks addressed specific interpretive skills based on learners' proficiency level (Novice, Intermediate, Pre-Advanced). For example, the Novice-level Interpretive Task assessed literal comprehension only; interpretive comprehension was assessed at the Intermediate and Pre-Advanced levels. In this second edition, this approach has been modified in light of current research on how the comprehension process occurs. The present-day view is that the listener/reader/viewer

constructs meaning of a text by using both bottom-up and top-down processing (Bernhardt, 1991; Swaffar, Arens, & Byrnes, 1991; Shrum & Glisan, 2010). In bottom-up processing, the learner arrives at meaning by analyzing language parts in a sequential manner (sounds/letters to form words, then words to form phrases, clauses, or sentences), while in top-down processing, the learner derives meaning "through the use of contextual cues and activation of background knowledge" (Shrum & Glisan, 2010, p.183). In sum, it is believed that both types of processing are used by the learner to understand and interpret a text. Further, learners use the knowledge and experiences that they bring to the text to derive meaning, including new insights gained in discussing texts with others (Bernhardt, 1991; Schmitt, Jiang, & Grabe, 2011). (See Chapter 6 of Shrum and Glisan, 2010, for a more in-depth discussion of the interpretive process.)

Students complete the interpretive task in the form of a "Comprehension Guide". See Appendix D for the revised IPA Interpretive Comprehension Guide Template. See Appendix E for the Comprehension Guide for "Why Do People Cross Borders?" (Troyan, 2008) as well as the corresponding authentic article for this IPA. The information acquired in the interpretive task is necessary for students to be able to complete the interpersonal task.

Interpretive Task
Intermediate Level
"Why Do People Cross Borders?"
You are leaving your country for Quebec. Before you leave your home country, you want to know more about values of the people of Québec. You need to consult pages 11 & 12 of *Apprendre le Québec*. A guide for new immigrants available online at
http://www.immigration-quebec.gouv.qc.ca/publications/fr/divers/apprendrelequebec.pdf
Read the guide and complete the accompanying "Comprehension Guide."

The "Comprehension Guide Analysis," shown in Figure 2.2, depicts the performance for students on a continuum from literal to interpretive comprehension. Notice that interpretive skills such as key word detection, main idea detection, and supporting detail detection are considered *literal comprehension tasks*, since they involve surface-level meaning. For these interpretive skills, learners will most likely all have the same or similar "literal" responses. On the other hand, the *interpretive comprehension tasks* require that learners are able to interpret, draw conclusions and infer deeper meanings from the text, i.e., read between the lines. Identifying organizational features of the text, guessing meaning in context, making inferences, and gleaning author/cultural perspectives are interpretive tasks that require inferencing skills. Inferencing has been defined as "a thinking process that involves reasoning a step beyond the text, using generalization, synthesis, and/or explanation" (Hammadou, 2002, p. 219). Wiggins (1998) reminds us that it may be impossible to assess our students' understanding of a text unless we discover the extent to which they know the author's intent, and by extension, cultural nuances underlying the text.

In the redefined approach presented in this second edition, interpretive tasks at each level engage learners in both literal and interpretive comprehension. The specific type of tasks and texts may vary according to the age, backgrounds, and sophistication of learners. For example, inferencing for a third grader might consist of anticipating what will happen next in a story, while for an adult learner it might consist of gleaning the author's viewpoint on an abstract topic through the text. To this end, the format used for the inferencing task may be tailored to the level of the learner, as indicated in the template that appears in Appendix D. See the description of the interpretive rubric later in this chapter for a more detailed discussion of the IPA assessment criteria for the interpretive mode of communication. Chapter Four presents a detailed discussion of how this view of the interpretive mode impacts the decision regarding selection of authentic texts.

Several points about conducting the interpretive phase should be kept in mind. First of all, since the purpose of the interpretive tasks is to assess learners' ability to deal with language that may be new for them in an authentic text, glossing or translating new words and expressions in the text should be avoided. Secondly, the use of translation from the target language to the native language should be avoided since this activity does not demonstrate one's ability to interpret a text and can lead to both frustration and boredom on the part of language learners. Finally, when the instructor

discusses the text with the class (both as a whole group and individually) in the feedback phase after the interpretive tasks have been done, students should be given an opportunity to analyze how accurate their contextual guessing was. This type of analysis will provide learners with helpful information regarding how successful their own contextual guessing is and how they might use this strategy more effectively.

Figure 2.2 Integrated Performance Assessment Comprehension Guide Analysis: Performance Expectations

CRITERIA	WHAT IS INVOLVED?
LITERAL COMPREHENSION	
Key word recognition	Students identify key words in the text that provide clues to the overall meaning of the text.
Main idea detection	Students identify the main idea(s) of the text.
Supporting detail detection	Students identify important details that further explain the main idea(s).
INTERPRETIVE COMPREHENSION	
Organizational features	Students identify the ways in which the text is organized and the purpose of organizing the information in that manner.
Guessing meaning from context	Students use contextual clues and knowledge of language and text structure to infer the meaning of new words and phrases.
Inferences (Reading between the lines)	Students interpret the overall meanings contained in the text by combining knowledge of key vocabulary, important details, text features, and their own background knowledge.
Author's perspective	Students identify the author's perspective and provide a justification.
Cultural perspectives	Students identify cultural perspectives/norms by connecting practices/products to cultural perspectives.

The Interpersonal Tasks

Interpersonal tasks are two-way, interactive activities such as face-to-face or telephone conversations and written correspondences where a back-and-forth exchange is expected such as e-mails or text messages. In oral interpersonal communication, speakers communicate in a spontaneous manner and do not use a written script.

In each IPA, students exchange information with each other, and express feelings, emotions, and opinions about the theme. Each of the two speakers comes to the task with information that the other person may not have, thereby creating a real need for students to provide and obtain information through the active negotiation of meaning. The information gathered during the interpersonal task is necessary to complete the presentational task that follows.

> **Interpersonal Task**
> **Intermediate Level**
> *"Why Do People Cross Borders?"*
> Based on what you have found out already about immigration and from your reading of the Culture section of Immigration Quebec's *Guide for New Immigrants,* you and a classmate explore ways that newcomers might have difficulty on their arrival. Come to consensus on at least three major areas of challenge newcomers face and provide examples or stories from any of your own or your family's experiences or background knowledge you have. (N.B. Students do not read any written notes during the interpersonal task. The interpersonal task is a spontaneous two-way interaction.)

The Presentational Tasks

Presentational tasks are generally formal speaking or writing activities involving one-way communication to an audience of listeners and readers, such as giving a speech or report, preparing a paper or story, or producing a newscast or video. In the IPA, students prepare a written or oral presentation based on the topic and information obtained in the previous two tasks. The written or spoken presentational tasks reflect what the students would do in the world outside the classroom. The intended audience includes someone other than the teacher, and the task avoids being merely an opportunity

to display language for the teacher. We recommend the presentational task as the culminating activity that results in the creation of a written or oral product.

> **Presentational Task**
> **Intermediate Level**
> *Why Do People Cross Borders?*
> Based on what you have learned, both in French and in the Humanities, about the experiences of individuals who chose to (or who are forced to) leave their countries, you will write a children's storybook about one person's story of immigration. You will present your stories at the Ecole Française du Maine in March.

A perusal of the thematically-based IPA tasks for the "Crossing Borders" theme highlights that Integrated Performance Assessment is an assessment rich in content that encourages learners to use a repertoire of linguistic skills and knowledge across the three modes of communication. Indeed to perform the tasks cited above, students will not be able to simply recite verb conjugations or memorized vocabulary lists. On the contrary, they will need to use the language with divergent and creative responses. Furthermore, learners will take risks and use language learning strategies, as well as critical thinking skills as they conceptualize, analyze, synthesize, interpret, make inferences, share opinions or exchange different points of view in the second language. In this way, IPA assessment is an integrative, dynamic and high-quality form of assessment.

Finally, by using an authentic document to launch the interpretive mode, the teacher may be able to interweave the cultural practices, products and perspectives of the Cultures goal area. This particular IPA addresses the Cultures Standard dealing with practices and perspectives. Through the reading for the interpretive task, the *practices* of the Québec government of recruiting French speakers to the province is revealed. Moreover, the general practices such as non-discrimination and the perspectives of overall values further reveal practices related to the ways in which citizens carry themselves. In uncovering these practices, students learn the *perspectives* of Québécois through the values of Québec's society summarized in the text. Besides the *Communication* and *Cultures* standards, this IPA also includes *Connections* (social studies and literature) and *Comparisons*. Furthermore, since students will share their stories with a French immersion school for the presentational task, this IPA addresses the *Communities* standard by engaging learners in meaningful use of language outside the boundaries of the classroom. See Chapter 6 for IPAs at the Novice, Intermediate, Intermediate High, and Advanced levels.

Selection of IPA Level for Use in the Classroom

Instructors will need to decide which level of the IPA would be most appropriate for their students. There is not a strict one-to-one match-up between the IPA level and the level of instruction of students; for example, an "Advanced Spanish" class may need to be given an Intermediate-level IPA. This determination should be based on the abilities of students according to the IPA rubrics (see next section) and the nature of classroom instruction and experiences, since the IPA is designed to form a seamless connection to instruction. Since the Novice-level IPA requires students to create with the language, it is advisable for students to be approaching Novice High proficiency so that they experience success with the IPA; i.e., they should be moving from using only memorized language to combining and recombining language elements on their own. A particular IPA level may be used for an entire year or even longer before progressing to a higher level IPA, depending on the progress students make (see next section for more details).

Integrated Performance Assessment Rubrics

Appendix F contains the revised IPA rubrics for use in scoring the tasks across the three modes of communication. As defined by Wiggins, a rubric is "a set of scoring guidelines for evaluating students' work" (1998, p. 154). Rubrics answer the following questions:

- By what criteria should performance be judged?

- Where should we look and what should we look for to judge performance success?

- What does the range in the quality of performance look like?

- How do we determine validity, reliability, and fairly judge what score should be given and what that score means?

- How should the different levels of quality be described and distinguished from one another? (Wiggins, 1998, p 154)

The three sets of IPA rubrics all contain *descriptors* for each level of performance. These rubrics are *generic* in nature—i.e., they describe characteristics of language performance without specifying particular content or task details; also, they are *analytic* inasmuch as they include a set of criteria for performance with a range of descriptions for each criterion (Center for Advanced Research in Language Acquisition [CARLA], 2012). In the IPA, rubrics serve the following purposes:

1. To inform learners of how they will be assessed prior to the assessment—i.e., what the performance expectations are. Instructors are encouraged to share models or exemplars of student work with learners together with performance rubrics in preparation for the IPA.

2. To provide descriptive feedback to learners along the continuum of performance so that they understand their current level of performance and what they need to do to improve.

3. To illustrate to learners how they might exceed or go beyond task expectations and therefore challenge themselves to improve (note that each rubric includes in the range of performance an "Exceeds Expectations" level).

4. To provide educators with a model to adjust performance expectations in light of student exemplars.

The format of each ready-to-use IPA rubric includes space for the instructor to provide a printed description of the student's evidence of strengths, areas in which improvement is needed, and any other comments that might assist the learner in making progress. A brief description of the rubrics for each mode follows and includes a discussion of how learners might demonstrate progress in interpretive, interpersonal, and presentational communication through their performance across multiple IPAs over time.

IPA Interpretive Rubric

As mentioned earlier, the nature of both the interpretive tasks and rubrics has been re-conceptualized in this second edition of the manual. The approach to the interpretive tasks has been discussed earlier: in short, we have embraced the current research indicating that the interpretive skills do not develop in a linear manner but rather involve the use of both top-down and bottom-up processing in concert. Since interpretive listening, reading, and viewing do not develop in the same manner as do speaking and writing, we have developed the view that the interpretive mode can be assessed along a continuum of performance. This new view of development in the interpretive mode of communication includes both literal and interpretive comprehension, according to the findings of literacy research and the new Common Core State Standards (ACTFL, 2012a; National Governors Association Center for Best Practices [CCSSO], 2010). Furthermore, this continuum of literacy development is the same regardless of the linguistic level/age of the learner. Although a single interpretive mode rubric is now used, most of the same criteria of the original interpretive rubrics have remained intact. The revised IPA interpretive rubric assesses the following aspects of performance (described in detail in Figure 2.2):

Literal Comprehension:
- Word Recognition
- Main Idea Detection
- Supporting Detail Detection

Interpretive Comprehension:
- Organizational Features
- Guessing Meaning from Context
- Inferences (Reading between the Lines)
- Author's Perspective
- Cultural Perspectives

This approach parallels the design of the interpretive rubric in the Framework for the Foreign Language National Assessment of Educational Progress originally proposed for 2004 (Center for Applied Linguistics, 2000). Further, it reflects the conceptualization of the interpretive process as illustrated in reading/language arts (Kamil, Pearson, Moje, & Afflerbach, 2011).

The rubrics describe a range of performance across a four-part continuum: Accomplished Comprehension—Exceeds expectations, Strong Comprehension—Meets Expectations (Strong), Minimal Comprehension—Meets Expectations (Minimal), Limited Comprehension—Does Not Meet Expectations. At each level in which the IPA is used (Novice,

Intermediate, etc.), learners will demonstrate progress in the interpretive mode as they move from "meeting expectations" to "exceeding expectations" over the course of a series of IPAs. It may take a year or two working at one IPA level to see consistent progress across the rubric categories! As learners advance to a higher level of IPA tasks, at first they may perform at a higher level on the literal tasks than on the interpretive tasks, but as students gain experience in interpreting authentic texts at the new level, their interpretive (i.e., inferencing) skills should also improve. In sum, use of this continuum over time will illustrate students' progress in developing both literal and interpretive comprehension with a variety of texts and within a variety of contexts.

IPA Interpersonal Rubrics

The rubrics designed to assess the IPA interpersonal tasks rate the following aspects of performance:

1. **Language Function:** language tasks the speaker is able to handle in a consistent, comfortable, sustained, and spontaneous manner; e.g., posing questions to a restaurant waiter/waitress to make a decision regarding what food to order.

2. **Text Type:** Quantity and organization of language discourse, on a continuum from words to phrases to sentences to connected sentences to paragraphs to extended discourse.

3. **Communication Strategies:** The quality of engagement and interactivity in the conversation; the amount of negotiation of meaning—i.e, strategies for clarifying meaning in the face of breakdown in communication; how one participates in the conversation and advances it.

4. **Comprehensibility:** Who can understand this person's language? Can this person be understood only by sympathetic listeners used to the speech of language learners? Can a native speaker unaccustomed to non-native speech understand this speaker?

5. **Language Control:** Grammatical accuracy, appropriate vocabulary, degree of fluency.

It is important to note that these criteria are aligned with both the performance domains in the *ACTFL Performance Descriptors for Language Learners* (2012b) as well as the assessment criteria in the *ACTFL Proficiency Guidelines* (2012c).

For each level (Novice, Intermediate, Intermediate-High, and Advanced), the rubrics describe a range of performance across a four-part continuum: Exceeds Expectations, Meets Expectations-Strong, Meets Expectations-Minimal, Does Not Meet Expectations. These descriptors of performance reflect progress according to the abilities described in the *ACTFL Proficiency Guidelines—Speaking* (ACTFL, 2012c); that is, the rubric at each IPA level (Novice, Intermediate, etc.) features overall performance that corresponds to the ACTFL guidelines. It is critical to note, however, that while one can discuss a student's performance at a particular proficiency level with respect to performance on IPAs, a student's specific level of oral proficiency cannot be determined on the basis of IPA tasks, but rather it can only be determined by an official Oral Proficiency Interview (OPI). Students demonstrate their ability to perform at a particular IPA level in the Interpersonal Mode when they can consistently perform across the criteria at the "Meets Expectations-Strong" point over the course of a series of IPAs, which may take a whole year or longer! Learners illustrate progress at a particular IPA level in the interpersonal mode when their performance moves across the rubric from meeting expectations at a minimal level to exceeding expectations of the level; this progress may also take significant time over the course of multiple IPAs.

IPA Presentational Rubrics

The rubrics designed to assess the IPA presentational tasks rate the following aspects of performance; it should be noted that all but one are the same as in the interpersonal rubrics:

> 1. **Language Function:** language tasks the speaker is able to handle in a consistent, comfortable, sustained, and spontaneous manner.
>
> 2. **Text Type:** Quantity and organization of language discourse, on a continuum from words to phrases to sentences to connected sentences to paragraphs to extended discourse.
>
> 3. **Impact:** The clarity, organization, and depth of the presentation and the degree to which the presentation maintains the attention and interest of the audience.
>
> 4. **Comprehensibility:** Who can understand this person's language? Can this person be understood only by sympathetic listeners used to the speech of language learners? Can a native speaker unaccustomed to non-native speech understand this speaker?
>
> 5. **Language Control:** Grammatical accuracy, appropriate vocabulary, degree of fluency.

As mentioned above in the case of the interpersonal rubrics, the criteria of the presentational rubrics are also aligned with the *ACTFL Performance Descriptors for Language Learners* (2012b) and the *ACTFL Proficiency Guidelines* (2012c).

The presentational rubrics include the criterion of *impact,* as described by Wiggins (1998) as characteristics of a performance that bring about a response from the audience of listeners/readers/viewers and/or holds their interest; i.e., in assessing impact, one might ask whether the performance is "powerful, memorable, provocative, or moving" (p. 67). While traditionally oral and written tasks have been evaluated primarily on linguistic accuracy, it is pivotal that authentic tasks such as those found in the IPA be assessed on the impact that the performances would have on a real-world audience beyond that of the classroom instructor. The *ACTFL Performance Descriptors for Language Learners*, in the communication strategies for the presentational mode, provide examples of how students might demonstrate impact.

The rubrics describe a range of performance across a four-part continuum: Exceeds Expectations, Meets Expectations-Strong, Meets Expectations-Minimal, Does Not Meet Expectations. The performance descriptors reflect progress according to the abilities described in both the *ACTFL Proficiency Guidelines* for both speaking and writing (ACTFL, 2012c), since the presentations may reflect tasks involving either speaking or writing. As indicated above with the interpersonal rubrics, a student's specific level of proficiency in presentational speaking or writing cannot be determined on the basis of IPA tasks, but rather it can only be determined by an official ACTFL Oral Proficiency Interview (OPI) for speaking and by an official ACTFL Writing Proficiency Test (WPT) for writing. Students demonstrate through an IPA their ability to perform at a particular level in the presentational mode when they can consistently perform across the criteria at the "Meets Expectations-Strong" point over the course of a series of IPAs, which may take a whole year or longer! Learners illustrate progress at a particular IPA level in the presentational mode when their performance moves across the rubric from meeting expectations at a minimal level to exceeding expectations of the level; this progress may also take significant time over the course of multiple IPAs.

Since the first edition of the IPA Manual, the interpersonal and presentational rubrics have been changed to add more descriptive language to the performance descriptions and to add rubrics for the Advanced-level learners, especially for those at the post-secondary level.

Adapting the IPA Rubrics for Specific Learning Contexts

As indicated above, the IPA rubrics across the modes are generic. Instructors may find it advantageous to adapt the rubrics for the following two purposes:

1. To make them more specific to performance expected in particular IPA tasks.

2. To make them more learner-friendly, appropriate to the age and linguistic level of learners; e.g., elementary-school learners may need rubrics that use simpler language that they can more easily understand. For example, as explained in Chapter 3, Davin, Troyan, Donato, and Hellmann (2011) found it necessary to revise the language of the IPA rubrics to make them clearer and more meaningful to younger learners.

However, instructors are cautioned to make every effort to maintain the integrity of the original IPA rubrics while making adaptations that are deemed necessary.

Using the IPA Rubrics to Evaluate or Assign Grades

Although rubrics are best used for purposes of communicating expectations to learners, describing learner progress, and providing meaningful feedback to learners, the reality of our educational system is that the use of rubrics must somehow result in scores or grades. It is likely that individual school districts and university language departments have their own systems of converting rubric results to grades. However, in the absence of such systems, instructors may find it helpful to assign a point-value to each column on the four-part continuum of performance on the rubric. For example, the "Exceeds" performance could be assigned 4 points, the "Meets—Strong" could be assigned 3 points, the "Meets—Minimal" would carry 2 points, and the "Does Not Meet" would carry 1 point. Figure 2.3 depicts the IPA Interpersonal Rubric—Novice Learner with these point values assigned to it.

In an analytic rubric that includes an "exceeds expectations" level of performance, a special conversion formula is typically used to assign percentages or points to the final score. It is essential for instructors to remember that raw scores on these rubrics cannot be converted directly to percentages, as this would, for example, result in assigning low grades to students who have "met expectations" on the task. A student receiving "Meets Expectations-Minimal" in each of the five categories would receive a raw score of 10 out of 20 total possible, or 50% or failure on most grading scales, which is hardly the right message for "Meets Expectations." As an example of how to carefully evaluate the raw score, if a student earned 3 points in each criterion of the rubric shown in Figure 2.3, the total raw score would be 15 out of 20. If straight percentage is used to assign a grade, the result would be a 75%, although the student "met expectations at the strong level." Many school districts, such as the Fairfax County (VA) Public Schools, have developed a system for converting rubric scores to grades (see *http://www.fcps.edu/is/worldlanguages/pals/documents/ConversionChart.pdf*). Because it is not possible for students to score a zero on a rubric, instructors must decide what the minimum passing score would be (e.g., 60%); as explained by Shrum and Glisan, "a mathe-

Figure 2.3 Integrated Performance Assessment (IPA) Interpersonal Mode Rubric—Novice Learner—With Scoring Points

CRITERIA	Exceeds Expectations 4	Meets Expectations Strong 3	Minimal 2	Does Not Meet Expectations 1
Language Function Language tasks the speaker is able to handle in a consistent, comfortable, sustained, and spontaneous manner	Creates with language by combining and recombining known elements; is able to express personal meaning in a basic way. Handles successfully a number of uncomplicated communicative tasks in straightforward social situations, primarily in concrete exchanges and topics necessary for survival in target-language cultures.	Uses mostly memorized language with some attempts to create. Handles a limited number of uncomplicated communicative tasks involving topics related to basic personal information and some activities, preferences, and immediate needs.	Uses memorized language only, familiar language.	Has no real functional ability.
Text Type Quantity and organization of language discourse (continuum: word - phrase - sentence - connected sentences - paragraph - extended discourse)	Uses simple sentences and some strings of sentences.	Uses some simple sentences and memorized phrases.	Uses words, phrases, chunks of language, and lists.	Uses isolated words.
Communication Strategies Quality of engagement and interactivity; how one participates in the conversation and advances it; strategies for negotiating meaning in the face of breakdown of communication	Responds to direct questions and requests for information. Asks a few appropriate questions, but is primarily reactive. May try to restate in the face of miscommunication.	Responds to basic direct questions and requests for information. Asks a few formulaic questions but is primarily reactive. May clarify by repeating and/or substituting different words.	Responds to a limited number of formulaic questions. May use repetition or resort to English.	Is unable to participate in a true conversational exchange.
Comprehensibility Who can understand this person's language? Can this person be understood only by sympathetic listeners used to interacting with non-natives? Can a native speaker unaccustomed to non-native speech understand this speaker?	Is generally understood by those accustomed to interacting with non-natives, although repetition or rephrasing may be required.	Is understood with occasional difficulty by those accustomed to interacting with non-natives, although repetition or rephrasing may be required.	Is understood, although often with difficulty, by those accustomed to interacting with non-natives.	Most of what is said may be unintelligible or understood only with repetition.
Language Control Grammatical accuracy, appropriate vocabulary, degree of fluency	Is most accurate when producing simple sentences in present time. Pronunciation, vocabulary, and syntax are strongly influenced by the native language. Accuracy decreases as language becomes more complex.	Is most accurate with memorized language, including phrases. Accuracy decreases when creating and trying to express personal meaning.	Accuracy is limited to memorized words. Accuracy may decrease when attempting to communicate beyond the word level.	Has little accuracy even with memorized words.

matical equation then converts the rubric points to a range of percentages between the highest possible—100% and the lowest possible—e.g., 60%" (2010, p. 417). Using this type of system, the following rubric formula could be used to assign a percentage:

(Total points x 52)/20 + 48 = _____%.

In the example provided above, a total raw score of 15 out of 20 would result in 87%, which is typically a high B and appropriately corresponds to the rubric label of "Meets Expectations-Strong." Instructors may also consult a Web site called Roobrix (*http://www.roobrix.com*), which calculates the score based on the number of criteria and the lowest passing grade entered by the instructor. Post-secondary institutions, such as Indiana University of Pennsylvania, have also adopted this system for converting rubric scores to grade percentages.

Instructors will find it helpful, if not necessary, to explain to their students how rubrics work, particularly if students are used to other formulas for assigning scores or grades. It bears mentioning that students do not need to reach "Exceeds" in each criterion to earn the grade of "A" since this category represents performance that is beyond what is expected on the IPA. As discussed above, the "Exceeds" column is to illustrate what learners need to do to improve their performance beyond what is expected by most learners on the task. Anecdotal reports from instructors who begin to use this type of rubric have revealed that many of their students work diligently because they want to exceed expectations once they see the criteria described on the rubric.

IPA Performance and Co-Constructive Feedback

Feedback is an integral part of IPA assessment since the main purpose or function of the assessment is *to improve language performance across the modes of communication.* Wiggins (1998) recommends that learners receive feedback as soon as possible after their performances. Effective feedback will assist the learners with knowledge and strategies for how they can improve their performance. We need to underscore that there is a critical difference between *evaluation* and *feedback,* as Miser (2007) explains: "Feedback is an objective description of a student's performance intended to guide future performance. Unlike evaluation, which judges performance, feedback is the process of helping learners to assess their performance, identify areas where they are on

target, and provide them tips on what they can do in the future to improve in areas that need improvement" (p.1). Citing numerous research studies, Bellon, Bellon and Blank (1992) stress that "Academic feedback is more strongly and consistently related to achievement than any other teaching behavior....This relationship is consistent regardless of grade, socioeconomic status, race or school setting" (p.227). Adair-Hauck (2000) suggests a co-constructive approach to IPA feedback, which can be characterized as an interactive, instructional dialogue between students (apprentices) and teacher (expert). Co-constructive IPA feedback encourages an active role of the learners to self-reflect, self-assess and peer-assess. See Chapter 5 for an in-depth discussion on research regarding the power of feedback, as well as characteristics and samples of instructional dialogues of co-constructive IPA feedback.

Summary: Unique Features of the ACTFL Integrated Performance Assessments (IPAs)

1. All three modes of communication (interpretive, interpersonal and presentational) are evaluated as an integrated unit of assessment, maintaining the same theme throughout the tasks;

2. IPAs are performance-based, providing learners with opportunities to perform meaningful, motivating and age-appropriate tasks;

3. IPAs are authentic assessments because they reflect real-world-tasks;

4. IPAs are developmental in nature (demonstrating cognitive and language development), as illustrated by the four levels of tasks in the interpersonal and presentational modes (Novice, Intermediate, Intermediate High and Advanced) and the various levels of interpretive abilities in the interpretive mode;

5. The IPA framework supports the seamless connection between instruction and assessment (see Chapter 4 for discussion);

6. Modeling of student performance is an integral part of the IPA framework (see Chapter 5 for discussion);

7. Co-constructive feedback that encourages learners to self-reflect and self-assess is a critical feature of IPA assessment (see Chapter 5 for discussion).

References

Adair-Hauck, B. (2000). *Exploring a socially-constructed approach to feedback and Integrated Performance Assessment.* Lecture presented at the University of Pittsburgh. Pittsburgh, PA.

Adair-Hauck, B. & Troyan, F. J. (2013). A descriptive and co-constructive approach to IPA assessment. *Foreign Language Annals, 46,* 23-44.

American Council on the Teaching of Foreign Languages (ACTFL). (2012a). *Alignment of the National Standards for Learning Languages with the Common Core State Standards.* Alexandria, VA: Author. Retrieved from http://www.actfl.org/sites/default/files/pdfs/Aligning_CCSS_Language_Standards_v6.pdf

American Council on the Teaching of Foreign Languages (ACTFL). (2012b). *ACTFL performance descriptors for language learners.* Alexandria, VA: Author.

American Council on the Teaching of Foreign Languages (ACTFL). (2012c). *ACTFL Proficiency Guidelines-Speaking, Writing, Listening and Reading,* 3rd ed. Alexandria, VA: Author.

Bellon, J. J., Bellon, E. C. & Blank, M.A. (1992). *Teaching from a research knowledge base: A development and renewal process.* New York: Macmillian Publishing Company.

Bernhardt, E. B. (1991). A psycholinguistic perspective on second language literacy. *Association Internationale de la Linguistique Apliquée Review, 8,* 31–44.

Center for Advanced Research in Language Acquisition (CARLA) Virtual Assessment Center (VAC). (2012). *Types of Rubrics.* Retrieved from http://www.carla.umn.edu/assessment/vac/Evaluation/p_6.html.

Center for Applied Linguistics (CAL). (2000). *Framework for the 2004 Foreign Language National Assessment of Educational Progress (NAEP).* Retrieved from http://www.nagb.org/publications/frameworks/FinalFrameworkPrePubEdition1.pdf.

Davin, K., Troyan, F. J., Donato, R., & Hellmann, A. (2011). Research on the Integrated Performance Assessment in an early foreign language learning program. *Foreign Language Annals 44,* 605-625.

Galloway, V. (1992). Toward a cultural reading of authentic texts. In H. Byrnes (Ed.), *Languages for a multicultural world in transition,* Northeast Conference Reports (pp.87-121), Lincolnwood, IL: NTC/Contemporary Publishing Company.

Glisan, E. W., Adair-Hauck, B., Koda, K., Sandrock, S. P., & Swender, E. (2003). *ACTFL Integrated Performance Assessment.* Yonkers, NY: ACTFL.

Hammadou, J. A. (2002). Advanced foreign language readers' inferencing. In J. A. Hammadou Sullivan (Ed.), *Literacy and the second language learner* (pp. 217–238). Greenwich, CT: Information Age Publishing.

Kamil, M. L., Pearson, P. D., Moje, E. B., Afflerbach, P. P. (2011). *Handbook of reading research: Volume IV.* New York, NY: Taylor & Francis.

Miser, W. F. (2007). Providing students with effective feedback. *Academic Leadership, The Online Journal, 4*(4).

National Governors Association Center for Best Practices, Council of Chief State School Officers (CCSSO). *Common Core State Standards for English Language Arts and Literacy in History/Social Studies, Science, and Technical Subjects.* (2010). Washington, DC: Author.

National Standards in Foreign Language Education Project (NSFLEP). (1996). *Standards for foreign language learning: Preparing for the 21st century (SFLL).* Lawrence, KS: Allen Press.

National Standards in Foreign Language Education Project (NSFLEP). (1999). *Standards for foreign language learning in the 21st century (SFLL)*. Lawrence, KS: Allen Press.

National Standards in Foreign Language Education Project (NSFLEP). (2006). *Standards for foreign language learning in the 21st century (SFLL)*. Lawrence, KS: Allen Press.

Schmitt, N., Jiang, X., & Grabe, W. (2011). The percentage of words known in a text and reading comprehension. *The Modern Language Journal, 95,* 26-43.

Shrum, J. L., & Glisan, E. W. (2010). *Teacher's handbook: Contextualized language instruction. 4th ed.* Boston, MA: Heinle Cengage Learning.

Swaffar, J., Arens, K., & Byrnes, H. (1991). *Reading for meaning.* Englewood Cliffs, NJ: Prentice Hall.

Troyan, F. J. (2008). *Rehearsal and feedback protocols for the IPA Interpersonal phase.* Paper presented at the American Council of Teaching of Foreign Languages.

Wiggins, G. (1998). *Educative assessment.* San Francisco: Jossey-Bass.

Chapter 3

Research on the Integrated Performance Assessment: A Historical Perspective

The IPA was originally designed in 1997 as a result of a U.S. Department of Education International Research and Studies grant received by ACTFL. The grant-funded project had three goals:

1. To develop an assessment prototype that would measure students' progress in meeting the *Standards for Foreign Language Learning in the 21st Century* (National Standards in Foreign Language Education Project, 1999, 2006);

2. To conduct research on the effectiveness of the assessment in measuring students' progress towards the Standards; and

3. To use the assessment to prompt curricular and instructional reform (Adair-Hauck, Glisan, Koda, Swender, & Sandrock, 2006).

During the three-year grant, a team of foreign language educators and assessment specialists designed the IPA and delivered professional development on the IPA to participating language teachers at six pilot sites located in Massachusetts, Pennsylvania, Virginia, Oklahoma, Wisconsin, and Oregon. The teachers also received training on the Oral Proficiency Interview (OPI) or the Modified Oral Proficiency Interview (MOPI). The IPA was piloted by some forty language teachers and approximately 1,000 students of Chinese, French, German, Italian, Latin, and Spanish across grade levels 3–12. After each of three rounds of field testing the IPA for purposes of researching its effectiveness as an assessment, revisions were made to the assessment and rubrics, performance data were compiled, and both teachers and students responded to questionnaires to share their perceptions of the IPA in terms of its usefulness and feasibility.

The results of the initial IPA project illustrated that the IPA had a "washback effect" on instruction—that is, it prompted teachers to modify their classroom practices to enhance their students' performance (Adair-Hauck et al., 2006). More specifically, teachers indicated that the IPA:

served as a catalyst to make them more aware of the need to integrate the three modes of communication into their lessons on a regular basis, design standards-based interpretive tasks using authentic documents, integrate more interpersonal speaking tasks, use more open-ended speaking tasks, and use more standards-based rubrics to help the students improve their language performance (Adair-Hauck et al., 2006, p. 373).

Of interest is that teachers reported that the challenges of implementing this type of performance-based assessment included the lack of age-appropriate authentic texts and the difficulty of preparing students for oral interpersonal tasks in which they would have to be spontaneous rather than read from a prepared text.

The IPA was subsequently researched at the post-secondary level to examine its feasibility beyond K-12 settings and to analyze student performance across the three modes of communication. A study undertaken at the U.S. Air Force Academy with cadets in an advanced Spanish course on Latin American Culture and Civilization specifically sought to discover how many students, exceeded, met, and did not meet communication expectations across the modes and to determine the extent to which secondary and post-secondary language study influenced their performance (Glisan, Uribe, & Adair-Hauck, 2007). This study marked the first instance of a video text being used in the interpretive mode, given that the early IPA project used only printed texts. In terms of the modes of communication, results of this investigation revealed that:

- students performed best on the presentational task, presumably because this mode has historically been the predominant mode in language classrooms;

- the interpretive mode was the only mode in which some cadets did not meet expectations, perhaps due to the fact that they reported having had more traditional secondary language classes that did not expose them to listening strategies;

- students did not perform as well on the interpersonal task as on the presentational task, which confirmed the anecdotal findings of the earlier project regarding the challenge of teaching spontaneous face-to-face communication;

- there was a positive correlation between years of language study in middle school and performance in the interpersonal mode—that is, students who studied language in middle school performed better on the interpersonal task; and

- there was a surprising negative correlation between years of language study in high school and performance across the three modes of communication, possibly pointing to students' traditional grammar-based courses and their lack of focus on meaningful communication (Glisan, Uribe, & Adair-Hauck, 2007).

Data from this post-secondary study also point to the possibility that the IPA may have a positive impact on learners' level of motivation to study a language and on their perceptions about language learning, although this remains to be confirmed in future research (Adair-Hauck, Glisan, & Uribe, in progress).

More recently, research has been undertaken on the IPA with students in the elementary school. Davin, Troyan, Donato, and Hellman (2011) studied the implementation of the IPA in a class of students in grades 4 and 5 who had studied Spanish for four years. As in the Air Force Academy project, this study incorporated a video segment in the interpretive task. Results of this investigation corroborate some of the earlier findings on studies of the IPA. In a comparison of performance across the three modes, data revealed that students received lowest ratings on the interpretive task, which reflects the same results obtained in the Air Force Academy study. The authors hypothesize that these results may be a consequence of a lack of exposure of students to authentic spoken texts and the presence of a large amount of unfamiliar vocabulary in the video segment (Davin et al., 2011). Another similarity between these two studies is that students in both contexts responded quite positively to the IPA on a follow-up survey, and both groups reported that

they enjoyed the opportunity to interact orally with their classmates in the interpersonal task. Finally, this elementary-school study revealed a positive washback effect on instruction, which corroborates the initial IPA investigation (Adair-Hauck et al., 2006).

The Davin et al. (2011) study also led to the following insights regarding use of the IPA in elementary grades:

- An outcome of the IPA is a metacognitive awareness on the part of the students of their own process of language learning. In this project, students were accurately able to assess their own abilities on the interpretive and presentational tasks of the IPA. Additionally, they demonstrated an understanding of the seamless connection between classroom activities and the IPA as an assessment. Further, they recognized the types of knowledge and experiences that they needed to progress and perform at a higher level.

- Students who speak languages in addition to English at home may be at an advantage on the IPA, as demonstrated in this study by students' performance on the interpersonal task. This corroborates existing research regarding the fact that students who learn multiple languages draw upon well-developed strategies and metalinguistic awareness (Sapienza, Donato, & Tucker, 2006).

In addition, two areas emerged that have helped to shape the current revision of the IPA Manual. First, the Davin et al. (2011) study revealed a significant correlation between the interpersonal and presentational tasks of the IPA; that is, there seems to be consistency between performance across these modes. However, the authors described a "discontinuity between the interpretive task and the other two tasks of the IPA," illustrating that the integrated use of the three modes of communication in this assessment does not imply that performance across the modes is parallel (Davin et al., 2011, p. 613). Secondly, the authors of the elementary-school IPA investigation found it necessary to revise the language of the IPA rubrics to make them clearer and more meaningful to younger learners.

As discussed above, the IPA has been researched since its inception at the elementary, secondary, and post-secondary levels to examine a number of different research questions, from those pertaining to learner performance to others focusing on the washback effect on instruction. In all of these studies regardless of the instructional level, the result that consistently emerged was that the IPA effectively merged assessment and instruction to the point that the instructors made significant modifications to their teaching and began "thinking like assessors" by turning their thinking to the specific results they expected students to achieve before instructional experiences were planned (Wiggins & McTighe, 2005, p. 150). Also, they changed their classroom activities and instructional approaches to improve learner performance. As an example, many teachers incorporated reading strategies to help their students deal with authentic texts and they provided more opportunities to rehearse spontaneously for oral interpersonal tasks (Adair-Hauck et al., 2006).

The initial three-year grant secured in 1997 to develop the IPA led to the publication of the first edition of the *ACTFL Integrated Performance Assessment Manual* (Glisan, Adair-Hauck, Koda, Sandrock, & Swender, 2003) and was soon followed by scholarly publications and teacher preparation materials that address the IPA (Sandrock, 2010; Shrum & Glisan, 2010), and even a video segment in the popular Annenberg/CPB video library, *Teaching Foreign Languages K-12: A Library of Classroom Practices* (WGBH Educational Foundation, 2003). The IPA also formed the basis for many of the segments in the Wisconsin Educational Communications Board series *World Language Assessment: Get in the Mode!* (2008). Since the inception of the IPA, language instructors K–16 have learned how to implement IPAs by participating in professional development opportunities offered by ACTFL at the annual ACTFL convention as well as through workshops delivered at their institutions. Language educators have developed IPAs and made them available online; for example, the Center for Advanced Research on Language Acquisition at the University of Minnesota has produced an impressive website with information on how to design an IPA and with a wealth of examples of IPAs in a number of different languages for K-16 classrooms (see Center for Advanced Research in Language Acquisition [CARLA], 2012).

An increasing number of school districts and universities have incorporated the IPA as a pivotal assessment in their language programs or have developed assessments based on the IPA construct. For example, in 2003, teachers in four districts in New Jersey participated in IPA training and began to create assessment tasks modeled after the IPA, with support from a Foreign Language Assistance Program (FLAP) grant. In 2009, this initial endeavor led to the development of a 21st century model unit that included an IPA as a summative assessment of the unit, and in 2012 the New Jersey Department of Education initiated a Model Curriculum Project, which will include the design of assessments modeled on the IPA. See Chapter 7 for additional details on these projects, including the impact of the IPA on teachers' assessment practices and on the teacher preparation programs at the post-secondary level.

It would be an understatement to say that there continues to be a growing interest in the field in the IPA. As illustrated in this description of the development of the IPA and research published on the assessment, it is clear that the IPA has:

1. filled the void for a performance based assessment that measures students' progress in meeting both the National Standards as well as proficiency levels as described in the *ACTFL Proficiency Guidelines;*

2. served as an avenue for promoting learners' metacognitive awareness of their language development as a result of the close connection between instruction and assessment and the cyclical approach to providing feedback;

3. prompted research and scholarly publications on this type of integrated assessment;

4. served as a catalyst for informing and improving classroom practice, assessment, and curricular design, not only for individual language teachers but also for school districts and states;

5. combined instruction and assessment in a seamless manner, thus responding to the call in current research for a more direct connection between teaching and assessment (McNamara, 2001);

6. raised additional questions regarding the relationship between and among the three modes of communication and ways in which rubrics can be designed to communicate performance expectations in clear and accessible ways for learners.

References

Adair-Hauck, B., Glisan, E. W., & Koda, K., Swender, E. B., & Sandrock, P. (2006). The Integrated Performance Assessment (IPA): Connecting assessment to instruction and learning. *Foreign Language Annals, 39*, 359-382.

Adair-Hauck, B., Glisan, E. W., & Uribe, D. (in progress). *Research on the Integrated Performance Assessment (IPA): Investigating Motivation and Perceptions of Language Learning and Assessment.*

Center for Advanced Research in Language Acquisition (CARLA) Virtual Assessment Center (VAC). (2012). *Types of Rubrics.* Retrieved from *http://www.carla.umn.edu/assessment/vac/CreatUnit/p_2.html*

Davin, K., Troyan, F. J., Donato, R., & Hellman A. (2011). Research on the Integrated Performance Assessment in an early foreign language learning program. *Foreign Language Annals 44,* 605-625.

Educational Communications Board. (2008). *World language assessment: Get in the mode!.* Madison, WI: Educational Communications Board. Retrieved from *http://www.ecb.org/worldlanguage assessment*

Glisan, E. W., Adair-Hauck, B., Koda, K., Sandrock, S. P., & Swender, E. (2003). *ACTFL Integrated Performance Assessment.* Yonkers, NY: ACTFL.

Glisan, E. W., Uribe, D., & Adair-Hauck, B. (2007). Research on Integrated Performance Assessment at the post-secondary level: Student performance across the modes of communication. *The Canadian Modern Language Review, 64,* 39-68.

McNamara, T. (2001). Language assessment as social practice: Challenges for research. *Language Testing, 18,* 334–399.

National Standards in Foreign Language Education Project (NSFLEP). (1999). *Standards for foreign language learning in the 21st century (SFLL).* Lawrence, KS: Allen Press.

National Standards in Foreign Language Education Project (NSFLEP). (2006). *Standards for foreign language learning in the 21st century (SFLL).* Lawrence, KS: Allen Press.

Sandrock, P. (2010). *The keys to assessing language performance.* Alexandria, VA: ACTFL.

Sapienza, B., Donato, R., & Tucker, G. R. (2006, October). Learning a second language: A district-wide foreign language program reaches the middle school. *The Language Educator, 1,* 24-27.

Shrum, J. L., & Glisan, E. W. (2010). *Teacher's handbook: Contextualized language instruction. 4th ed.* Boston, MA: Heinle Cengage Learning.

WGBH Educational Foundation. (2003). *Teaching foreign languages K-12: A library of classroom practices.* Burlington, VT: Annenberg/CPB.

Wiggins, G., & McTighe, J. (2005). *Understanding by design.* Alexandria, VA: Association for Supervision and Curriculum Development.

Chapter 4

Linking Assessment and Learning via IPA

Linking IPA and Instruction:
A Tool for Backward Design

The research on the IPA discussed in Chapter Three presents a clear case regarding the link between assessment and instruction. These studies (Adair-Hauck et al., 2006; Davin et al., 2011a; Glisan, Uribe, & Adair-Hauck, 2007) highlight the important role of instructional design that reflects the tasks and performances of the IPA; in other words, the IPA is only as good as the instruction that leads to it. This chapter links an example of the IPA from a high school French classroom to instructional activities. To illustrate this relationship between assessment and instruction, we present the IPA as a tool for backward planning according to *Understanding By Design* (referred to as UbD, Wiggins & McTighe, 2005).

Since the publication of *Understanding by Design* (Wiggins & McTighe, 2005), backward design has been promoted in the profession (Glisan, 2010; Glisan et al., 2003; Sandrock, 2010; Shrum & Glisan, 2010). Furthermore, the IPA was conceived as a tool for backward design of assessment and instruction (Glisan et al., 2003) and has been implemented as such (Davin, Troyan, Hellmann, & Donato, 2011a, 2011b; Fredericks-Malone & Gadbois, 2005/2006; Troyan, 2008; Troyan, Davin, Donato, & Hellmann, 2012). Backward design provides a framework for the planning and implementation of instruction that is linked to the Standards and the authentic performance tasks of the IPA.

Understanding by Design: A Framework
for Planning the IPA

To assist teachers in implementing this approach to instructional planning that is informed by and explicitly linked to performance assessment, Wiggins and McTighe (2005) provide a template that guides teachers through the three stages of UbD. This section presents an adapted version (see Figure 4.1) of the UbD template that incorporates the three tasks of the IPA into the three steps of the UbD to guide foreign language teachers in identifying:

1. Desired results—the standards addressed, the essential questions answered, the understandings uncovered, and the language, content, and performances developed;

2. Assessment evidence—formative and summative assessment tasks aligned with the desired results;

3. Learning activities in the sequence of instruction linked to the assessments.

It is important to note that in implementing backward design, a "unit" may be considered the traditional unit of instruction, a semester, or yearlong sequence of instruction (see Glisan, 2010, for a discussion). This section depicts a teacher's planning process in a combined French 3 and 4 classroom for an IPA linked to UbD (see Figure 4.2). The IPA and unit of instruction were designed to answer the essential question "Why Do People Cross Borders?" over the course of a three-month unit of instruction.

> **IPA Overview**
> **Intermediate Level**
> *"Why Do People Cross Borders?"*
> You are studying immigration in your community and beyond. This study has sparked your curiosity to learn as much as possible about the immigration experience. First, you will read about how the province of Québec welcomes newcomers and introduces them to the "fundamentals" of Québec society. Based on what you have found out already about immigration, you and a classmate explore ways that newcomers might have difficulty on their arrival. Finally, you will create a storybook about that newcomer's experience and read the book to students at a local French immersion school.

Step One—Identify Desired Results

In the first step, the teacher identifies the standards, the essential questions, and the overall objectives that the unit will address. These components comprise the targets or "desired results" of instruction. The process begins with the identification of the "Established Goals" or, as this example illustrates, the *Standards addressed* in the unit of instruction.

In the unit described here, the teacher identified the Communication Standards (interpersonal, interpretive, and presentational). It is important to note that the use of the IPA in the UbD framework to planning ensures that these three standards are part of assessment and, therefore, embedded in and practiced through the learning activities throughout the unit of instruction. In addition to the Communication Standards, the teacher identifies specific standards from Cultures, Connections, and Communities because the students will demonstrate an understanding of the relationship between the practices and perspectives of the cultures studies, acquire information and access diverse perspectives that are available through the language and its cultures, and use the language both within and beyond the school setting.

After the "Established Goals" have been articulated in the form of the Standards, the teacher unpacks the goals by identifying "Essential Questions" and the corresponding "Understandings." To determine the essential questions for the unit, the teacher identifies the "principles, laws, theories, or concepts" that need to be "uncovered" in the unit (Wiggins & McTighe, 2005). Each understanding is phrased to complete the sentence "Students will understand that…" For example, in this unit of instruction, the teacher wanted students to develop the understanding that "people migrate from one place to another for various reasons". To arrive at this understanding, students will investigate the essential question "Why do people choose to leave one place and settle in another?" Throughout the learning activities and performance assessments, students will learn that there are many reasons for which people leave one country for another: a desire to travel, an obligation to work, a forced exodus because of a human rights crisis. Based on the goals, questions, and understandings identified, the teacher completes the final component of Step One by identifying what students "will know" and "be able to do".

The former encompasses the knowledge about content and language that students will acquire during the unit. In this section, the teacher lists the important cultural knowledge (i.e., the communities around the world from which people came to Portland) that and key linguistic features (i.e., vocabulary and grammar). It is important to note that the "knowledge" identified in this section is bound to the content and contexts described in the Essential Questions

and Understandings sections. In particular, the linguistic knowledge identified here should be linked to the descriptions of what students will be able to do with language in the next column.

The latter describes the performance tasks in which students will apply that knowledge (Wiggins & McTighe, 2005). Here, the teacher lists the language functions that students will be asked to demonstrate. These statements should include a language function (interpret, talk, discuss, interview, describe) in one of the three modes of communication. In each case, the statements in this column should be linked back to what students "will know" in the previous column. Linking the information in the two columns in this way ensures that language learning is embedded in a meaningful context (Shrum & Glisan, 2010).

Step Two—Determine Acceptable Evidence
The second step involves the design of summative and formative assessments. In this step of the UbD template, the teacher describes the range of assessments in the unit. These assessments are divided into two types. The first type, summative assessment, is comprised of the performance tasks of IPA at the end of the unit. The second type, formative assessment, includes assessments serving as checkpoints throughout the unit of instruction. The formative assessments serve two purposes. In one respect, they provide critical data for the teacher, who uses it to inform and modify instruction (Black & Wiliam, 1998; Halverson, Pritchett, & Watson, 2007; Supovitz & Klein, 2003) by "uncovering the learners' *understandings and misunderstandings* all along the way" (Wiggins & McTighe, 2005, p. 247, italics in original). In another respect, some of the formative assessment tasks are intentionally designed to mirror the performance in the summative IPA, thereby providing a critical opportunity for modeling and practicing of performance (Adair-Hauck & Troyan, 2013; Tharpe & Gallimore, 1988; Wiggins, 1998). This layering of assessment types throughout the unit of instruction is becoming common in standards-based assessment in the United States and is increasingly employed in school- and district-wide decisions (Halverson, Pritchett, & Watson, 2007; Supovitz & Klein, 2003) and in language program reform (Byrnes, 2002).

In the unit highlighted in the example, the teacher identifies the summative performance tasks in one column. In another

Figure 4.1 Unit Planning Template Adapted for IPA

Stage 1—Desired Results

Established Goal(s)—Standards Addressed:

Essential Question(s):	**Understanding(s):** *Students will understand that…*
Students will know… **Key Cultural and Linguistic Knowledge**	*Students will be able to…* **Key Language Functions and Communication Strategies**

Stage 2—Assessment Evidence

Summative Integrated Performance Assessment (IPA) *The statements below later become IPA task overviews.*	**Formative Assessment Evidence**
Interpretive Mode: Interpersonal Mode: Presentational Mode:	Interpretive Mode: Interpersonal Mode: Presentational Mode: Other evidence:

Stage 3—Learning Plan

G. Wiggins and J. McTighe (2005). *Understanding by design* (expanded 2nd ed.). Alexandria, VA: Association for Supervision and Curriculum Development. Template adapted and reprinted with permission from the authors.

Figure 4.2 Unit Planning Template: IPA Example

Stage 1—Desired Results	
Established Goal(s)—Standards Addressed:	
Communication Standards (Interpersonal, Interpretive, Presentational) Cultures Standard (Relating Cultural Practices to Perspectives)	Connections Standard (Acquiring Information) Communities Standard (School and Community)
Essential Question(s): Why do people choose to leave one place and settle in another? Why do people choose to resettle in Portland, Maine? Were there people in my family who "crossed borders"? What are the Cultural "values" of different Francophone Communities?	**Understanding(s):** *Students will understand that…* People migrate from one place to another for various reasons. Many members of our community have very recently come from different locations around the world. In many ways, the hardships experienced by Franco-Americans in New England and Maine parallel the experiences of current refugees in our community.
Students will know… (Key Cultural and Linguistic Knowledge) • the communities around the world from which people came to Portland. • the reasons that they left their homes to come here. • key vocabulary, expressions, and grammar to engage in interpretive, interpersonal, and presentational tasks related to personal immigration stories. • the basics about how to use the passé compose and the *imparfait* in context.	*Students will be able to… (Key Language Functions and Communication Strategies)* • interpret a text about how Quebec welcomes immigrants to unpack the cultural values of the province. • interview members of the Portland community to understand the reasons for which they relocated to our city. • talk about the reasons why people "cross borders." • present stories about those immigration stories and respond to questions about them.
Stage 2—Assessment Evidence	
Summative Integrated Performance Assessment (IPA) *The statements below later become IPA task overviews.* Interpretive Mode: As part of your study on immigration, you want to learn about how different countries present their culture to new-comers. You decide to consult the text Apprendre le Québec, a publication of the Québec government for newcomers to the province. Read the excerpt from the publication and complete the accompanying "Comprehension Guide." Interpersonal Mode: Based on your study of immigration, you are interested to know about the experience of immigrants in your town/region/state. You have located a resident of (your town) who is from Senegal, part of the French-speaking world. Interview him/her about the experience of coming to the United States, finding a place to live, getting a job, etc. Presentational Mode: Based on what you have learned—both in French class and in Humanities–about the experience of individuals who chose to (or who were forced to) leave their countries, you will write a children's storybook about one person's story of immigration. You will present your stories to students at the French immersion school in March.	**Formative Assessment Evidence** Interpretive Mode: • Completion of a comprehension guide while listening to the song *Sunugaal* • Listening task connected to the song *Là-bas* • Reading other students' familial stories of immigration Interpersonal Mode: • On-going formative assessment tasks connected to the final interpersonal mode task (See Appendix G). • Information-gap tasks using a map detailing where certain Franco-American families lived in a local town. Presentational Mode: • Short class narrative presentations telling their familial stories of immigration Other Evidence: • Contextualized Close Quiz on the passé composé.

Figure 4.2 (continued) Unit Planning Template: IPA Example

Stage 3 —Learning Plan

Learning Activities:

1. Introduce the title of the unit; have the students brainstorm answers to the question.

2. Introduce the essential questions and the culminating IPA tasks.

3. At the beginning of each class, students participate in a practice conversation in which they play the role of a person from a different country (see Appendix G). Each day, I film one dyad to give the group formative feedback on their performance. Each day, after the practice, students list vocabulary that they needed but were unable to access (see Appendix H). Through these interactions and vocabulary building activities, students engage in active negotiation of meaning and learn new strategies to maintain interaction.

4. Tell the immigration story about my grandfather in French using the PACE Method (Adair-Hauck & Donato, 2010). Isolate and begin to analyze the tenses of the verbs.

5. A resident of Portland who is originally from Haiti describes his experience of immigrating to the United States and settling in Portland.

6. Students study the immigration of Franco-Americans to a nearby town and, using maps of the town, complete an information-gap activity about the town.

7. Students compose their familial story of immigration.

8. Students rehearse the presentation of their stories in small groups and receive feedback.

9. Students present their stories to another high school class in the district.

10. Students interpret the themes in the spoken word "Gibraltar" by the slammer Abd Al Malik.

11. Students complete an interpersonal task comparing and contrasting the themes in "Gibraltar" and those of residents of Maine that we have studied.

12. Students create, compare, and contrast the "portraits" of two individuals encountered in the study of immigration. In doing so, students link to universal themes across immigration experiences.

13. The Case Study of Québec. Through an interpretive reading task, students learn about the role of immigration in Québec.

14. IPA Interpretive Task

15. Interpretive Feedback Loop

16. IPA Interpersonal Task

17. Interpersonal Feedback Loop

18. IPA Presentational Task

19. Presentational Feedback Loop (in the form of structured in-class peer feedback on rehearsal)

20. Presentation of Storybooks at the French immersion school.

G. Wiggins and J. McTighe (2005). *Understanding by design* (expanded 2nd ed.). Alexandria, VA: Association for Supervision and Curriculum Development. Template adapted and reprinted with permission from the authors.

column, the teacher describes the formative performance tasks and other types of evidence (i.e., quizzes, writing prompts, interpretive reading and listening tasks, speaking tasks). Notice that the description of the summative performance tasks by mode of communication corresponds to the IPA task overviews that the students will receive before they complete each task. The formative assessments may include a range of assessment types; however, it is critical that some of the assessments in this column model the type of performance that will be required in the summative IPA. In other words, in addition to providing the teacher with data for instructional decisions, formative assessments allow students to engage in performances tasks that are analogous to the summative IPA tasks.

Step Three—Plan Learning Activities

Only after the goals for the unit have been established and the assessments designed can the teacher begin to plan instruction. This approach, in effect, is the opposite of the traditional approach to instructional planning in which a teacher would, as Wiggins describes, "teach, test and hope for the best" (Annenberg/CPB, 2004). By contrast, the learning activities that evolve in the UbD process are planned with "the end in mind" (Annenberg/CPB, 2004). Notice that the activities described engage students in meaningful communication that prepares them for the formative and summative performance assessment tasks. For example, to begin to prepare students for the summative interpersonal task on the IPA, the teacher designed an on-going learning activity to give them consistent practice engaging in the type of role playing that will be required during the IPA. This daily role-play also functions as a formative assessment, an opportunity for the student to self-assess his/her performance, and preparation for an authentic interview that they will later conduct with a newcomer.

As discussed above, the IPA will only be as effective as the instruction that leads to it. For this reason, the UbD approach to planning can assist teachers, districts, and programs in realizing the potential of the IPA to align assessment, instruction, and learning with the Standards (Adair-Hauck et al., 2006; Glisan et al., 2003). UbD offers a framework for planning that is aligned with the design features of the IPA (Glisan et al., 2003, p. 24). Through one sample IPA, this section has traced the steps of UbD, beginning with the articulation of goals as expressed in the Standards, continuing in the depiction of assessments in the unit, and culminating in a description of learning activities linked to the goals and assessments. To expand on this discussion of the planning of instruction and assessment, the following section outlines guidelines for teachers in planning IPAs, formative assessments, and the instructional activities linked to the IPA in the UbD approach to planning.

Considerations in the Preparation of Learning Activities

Learning Activities to Prepare Students for the Interpretive Task

Chapter Two presented a detailed discussion of the IPA interpretive tasks and the comprehension guide that students complete to illustrate their level of comprehension and interpretation. The tasks progress across levels from those that require *literal comprehension*—detection of key words, main ideas, and supporting details—to more *interpretive comprehension*—identification of organizational features, guessing meaning from context, gleaning inferences, and identifying author and cultural perspectives. Students need a great deal of experience in exploring authentic texts and acquiring strategies for how to derive meaning from them. Strategies such as skimming for the main idea and scanning for details will help students to understand the literal meaning of texts. It is essential that students realize that total comprehension of a text is not the goal and that translation from the target

language of the text into one's native language does not constitute comprehension or interpretation—in fact, translation is a strategy that should be discouraged in the interpretation process. Additionally, students should gain experience in engaging in interpretive comprehension by learning to use the context and organizational features of the text as clues to meaning as well as exploring with their classmates inferences, perspectives of the author, and cultural insights. Learners often gain new insights about a text as a result of text-based discussions that they have with their peers. This social view of the interpretive process reflects the sociocultural view of language learning, in which learners and the instructor co-construct meaning, and it "mirrors the way in which comprehension is constructed socioculturally in the world outside the classroom" (Shrum & Glisan, 2010, p. 184).

In sum, preparing students to comprehend and interpret an authentic text in the IPA requires a number of instructional strategies to give students confidence in dealing with the target language in its authentic form. Some specific strategies that the teacher might use include:

- integrating authentic texts into instruction on a regular basis;
- providing opportunities for students to explore an authentic text to glean either the main idea or specific details (skimming or scanning), but without having to demonstrate an understanding of the entire text;
- preparing students for the task by activating their background knowledge and engaging them in anticipating the main idea of what they will listen to/read/view;
- encouraging students to develop their own purposes for listening to / reading / viewing an authentic text;
- providing students with strategies for comprehending authentic printed texts such as using contextual clues, using word families as clues to figuring out the meaning of new words, identifying key words that provide clues to meaning, using titles and visuals that appear with the text as clues to meaning;
- providing opportunities for students to check their initial guesses about meaning against the context and revise them as necessary;

- providing students with strategies for comprehending authentic oral texts such as listening to the segment a number of times—each time for additional information, pausing the recorded segment to give time for recalling what was heard, listening for key words only;

- designing interpretive activities that include pair and group collaboration;

- using interpretive tasks as the basis for interpersonal and presentational communication;

- assisting students in moving from literal comprehension (key word, main idea and supporting detail detection) to interpretive comprehension (word and concept inferences, organizational principles, author, and cultural perspectives of the text);

- facilitating the interpretive task by enabling learners to collaborate with one another, construct meaning together, use teacher and peer feedback in refining their hypotheses, and accept an active role in developing their interpretive abilities; and

- providing opportunities for students to select their own authentic texts of interest and demonstrate their comprehension and interpretation of them (Shrum & Glisan, 2010).

Factors To Consider When Selecting Authentic Texts for the Interpretive Tasks

Another important aspect of preparing students for these interpretive tasks is the selection of the appropriate text for both classroom learning activities and use in the IPA (Glisan et al., 2003). Teachers can use various sources from the target language culture to find the texts (oral, printed, video) required for the interpretive tasks, both for the classroom practice that prepares students for the IPA and for the IPA itself. The texts selected should be *authentic*; that is, those texts "produced *by* members of a language and culture group *for* members of the same language and culture group" (Galloway, 1998, p. 133). While teachers may find it intuitively appropriate to "simplify" or "edit" authentic texts to make them easier for students to interpret, particularly for students in beginning language classes, research indicates that learners demonstrate a higher level of comprehension on texts that are read in their authentic, unedited versions in contrast to versions that are simplified through lexical

changes (e.g., substituting known vocabulary for original vocabulary contained in the text); see for example: Allen, Bernhardt, Berry, & Demel, 1988; Oguro, 2008; Young, 1999. Simplifying a text for learners may in reality be counterproductive, given that the natural redundancy of the authentic context facilitates comprehension (Shrum & Glisan, 2010). An alternative to changing the text and sacrificing its authenticity is to teach students strategies for interpreting authentic texts such as using their background knowledge, the context of the text, and word families to hypothesize meaning. It is important to evaluate the oral and printed texts included as part of a textbook program to judge if they are authentic or if they are prepared by the textbook authors merely for instructional purposes.

According to Shrum & Glisan (2010), there are two types of factors that should be taken into account when selecting an authentic text: 1) reader- and listener-based factors and 2) text-based factors. The following are several important research based findings that deal with *what the listener/reader/ viewer brings to the interpretive task:*

1. **Topic familiarity and Purpose for Listening/Reading/ Viewing:** Students will have greater success if the texts selected deal with topics with which they are familiar and if they are encouraged to establish a purpose for exploring these texts.

2. **Short-Term or Working Memory:** Teachers should be aware of the load on memory that students may experience during the comprehension task, and they should plan to control for this by allowing students to have the printed text available while completing a reading comprehension task and allowing students to listen to an oral text or view a video text multiple times.

3. **Strategies in Comprehending and Interpreting/Anxiety:** Students have more success in interpreting texts if they are taught to interact with the text through the use of both bottom-up processes (comprehending pieces of the text in a linear fashion) and top-down processes (interpreting the "whole," the big ideas of the text). Students' comprehension will increase if they are trained to use strategies such as activation of background knowledge, contextual guessing, and use of nonverbal cues, which will also serve to lessen their anxiety. Teachers should encourage students to self-report periodically while listening, reading, and

viewing so that teachers will be informed about the comprehension strategies their students are using (cited from Shrum & Glisan, 2010, pp. 199-200).

Selecting an appropriate text is no simple task, as the teacher must keep in mind several important considerations regarding *text-based factors:*

1. The text should be ***context*-appropriate:** Texts should reflect contexts and content areas that learners are exploring in the language class or program so that background knowledge can be activated. For example, a text on good nutrition habits would be context-appropriate within a unit on "maintaining a healthy lifestyle," while students are acquiring vocabulary on food, learning about food preparation and exercise, and exploring the perspectives of the target culture relative to staying healthy. Presentation of such a text in the absence of this contextual foundation would likely result in frustration for learners and lack of interest. In this vein, students' interest level has been found to be a key factor in text selection to the extent that students may be able to interpret at a higher level when the text is more interesting to them (Dristas & Grisenti, 1995).

2. The text should be ***age*-appropriate:** Learners in elementary school, for example, might not be able to relate to authentic soap operas, talk shows, or newspaper editorials, because cognitively these texts would be too complex and also would not capture the interest of a typical younger learner. At this age, learners might respond more effectively to stories, fairy tales, folktales, and legends; concrete descriptions of people and places; personal letters; conversations between young people or interviews. Likewise, adolescents might access texts dealing with issues connecting to their daily lives, such as making choices to deal with stress.

3. The text should be **appropriate for the *linguistic level*** of learners: This does not mean that teachers should select only texts that have the exact grammar and vocabulary that students have learned (this would be impossible anyway)!! It means that the text should have enough language that students can recognize so that they can use these recognizable portions on which to scaffold meaning. It bears mentioning that listeners/readers/viewers may pay more attention to words that carry content as opposed to

grammatical markers as in the case of verb endings, for example. An important factor to consider when selecting texts is the degree of contextual support. For example, longer texts may be easier for students to comprehend because they provide more of a context from which meaning may be interpreted. Additionally, the organization of the text may impact ease in interpretation; texts with story-like features (those that have a beginning, middle, and end) and signaling cues may facilitate comprehension. Linguistic signaling cues such as connector/transition words (e.g., *in addition to, on the other hand*) and non-linguistic signaling cues such as charts, graphs, pictures, or subtitles provide additional support to assist learners in drawing meaning from the text.

4. Learners should be able to have success in interpreting the text if the teacher ***edits the task* and not the text.** That is, teachers should take great care to design interpretive tasks that are appropriate to the linguistic level of learners, while challenging them to stretch and develop further their interpretive abilities.

In sum, instructors may find it helpful to remember the acronym "CALL-IT" to recall these text-based factors:

C	=	Context
A	=	Age
LL	=	Linguistic Level
IT	=	Importance of Task

Instructors are encouraged to consider the CALL-IT factors very closely as they select authentic texts and to "edit the task, not the text."

In the first edition of this manual, we presented a dichotomy of text types according to proficiency levels. In this second edition, we have re-conceptualized this discussion to acknowledge the fact that any text can be interpreted at a variety of linguistic levels. There is nothing inherent in the text itself to make it novice, intermediate, intermediate high, etc. It is the task that needs to be adapted to the learner's language level, not the text. Consequently, a given text is not static in terms of how it might be interpreted. What enables a text to be interpreted is what the listener/reader/viewer brings to the interpretive task—i.e., how the learner interacts with the text. For instance, some authentic travel brochures may be more accessible to readers than are others based on the factors described above. One caution is that some simple texts may not allow for a depth of understanding since the purpose is strictly to present charts of information to help the reader make a decision, such as airline schedules or menus.

Figure 4.3 depicts an authentic text that deals with a famous Spanish-speaking singer, found in the magazine *Okapi*, published in Spain for adolescents. This text would be appropriate for the Famous Person IPA, which could be integrated effectively into an instructional unit dealing with topics such as description of people/biographies, leisure-time activities, or professions. Within one of these units, the text would be context-appropriate and would build upon what students learned in terms of content and culture. Although the text could be used with learners at any level, it fits well within the Intermediate-level IPA, given the types of tasks that these learners should be able to do in the interpersonal and presentational modes. The text was selected with middle-school or high-school learners in mind, since they often read about idols in the film and music industries; hence it might be of personal interest to this group of learners. Having some vocabulary beyond the Novice level would be helpful in interpreting this particular text, which includes much language beyond simple vocabulary and cognates. Additionally, the text is graphically organized, with visuals, subtitles, use of different fonts and boxes—all of which entice the reader and facilitate the reader's comprehension and interpretation process.

The following is a list of the types of authentic texts that instructors might consider incorporating into work on the interpretive mode and into IPAs. It bears repeating that text selection should take into account the factors described above:

Some examples of interpretive listening/viewing tasks include but are not limited to:

- Interviews or surveys from youth-oriented TV programming;

- Straightforward conversations taped from a youth-oriented music program on TV or radio;

- Product commercials in the target language from TV or radio;

- Public service announcements on radio or TV such as the anti-smoking or anti-drug campaigns;

- Authentic songs* by artists of the target culture based on familiar contexts or theme being studied.

- Animated cartoons;

- Segments from soap operas or other television programming;

- Interviews from talk shows from the target cultures.

Songs created by textbook publishing companies or those that are "instructional" (such as those to remember verb forms) do not represent authentic listening tasks, as they are not real products of the target culture.

Some examples of interpretive reading tasks include but are not limited to:

- Personal letters or e-mail correspondence;

- Simple biographies or descriptions of people from a popular culture magazine or newspaper;

- Product commercials in the target language from newspaper or magazines;

- Public service announcements in magazines and newspapers such as anti-smoking or anti-drug campaigns;

- Product advertisements or sales advertisements from a supermarket.

- Interviews or surveys from youth-oriented magazines;

- Short stories;

- Advice columns of personal interest to students;

- Photo stories with captions such as the "fotonovelas";

- Essays or editorials in authentic target culture newspapers;

- Authentic songs or poetry by artists of the target culture;

- Comic strips.

Learning Activities to Prepare Students for the Interpersonal Task

During an interpersonal task, two students exchange information with each other, express feelings, emotions, and opinions about the theme or task. Each of the two speakers comes to the task with information that the other person

Figure 4.3 Laura Esquivel Authentic Text Spanish

Laura Esquivel

Mucho más que un "patito feo"
La serie de TV *Patito Feo* la ha convertido en un auténtico ídolo infantil. Pero, sin ella, seguramente esta actriz y cantante argentina también hubiera triunfado, gracias a su versatilidad y su gran talento.

¡Mamá, quiero ser artista!
Con apenas 7 años, Laura tenía bastante claro que quería ser artista, así que empezó a estudiar piano, canto, baile, e interpretación. Quizá algo de ese espíritu artístico lo había heredado de su abuelo, Horacio Esquivel, un pionero de la escenografía en Argentina. Y, por supuesto, no tardó en subirse a un escenario; en concreto para interpretar a Wendy y a un "Niño perdido" en el musical *Peter Pan. Todos podemos volar.*

Artista completa
Laura tenía 9 años, y ya comenzaba a ser considerada una de las artistas infantiles más populares de su país; bueno, y de otros como México, donde, en 2004, participó y ganó el *reality* musical para niños *Código FAMA Internacional.* Por aquel entonces, ya había hecho sus pinitos como actriz, cantante, presentadora…y había compartido escenario con artistas tan famosos como Belinda y Juanes, entre otros.

La dulce Patricia Castro
Después de una corta pero intensa carrera artística, su gran oportunidad de triunfar internacionalmente le llegó de la mano de Disney Channel, que la seleccionó para interpretar a la dulce y soñadora Patricia Castro, alias "Patito", en la serie *Patito feo.* "Aquella noticia – afirma – la recibí con una gran emoción; empecé a gritar en casa, ¡me sentí muy feliz!". Y no era para menos; esta comedia infantil, que se estrenó en 2007, pronto se convirtió en un auténtico fenómeno no solo en países como Argentina, México, Colombia, Venezuela, Paraguay…, sino también en Francia, Portugal, Italia…y, por supuesto, España, donde ya se ha estrenado la segunda temporada.

Más allá de "Patito"
Aunque ha estado de gira con su espectáculo Patito feo: el musical más bonito, con el que recorrió España este verano, Laura tiene claro que quiere olvidarse de la serie y hacer otras cosas. Por eso, este mismo año ha colaborado en programas de TV como *Mundo teen* (Argentina), *Cántame una canción* (España) y ha trabajado en la película italiana *Un paradiso per due,* un filme ecológico para toda la familia. En fin, que oportunidades de trabajar en lo que quiera no le van a faltar.

Ha dicho
"No haría telenovelas para adultos. A mí me gustan mucho los chicos/as y los adolescentes. A mi edad quiero hacer cosas de adolescentes. No quiero quemar etapas".

Ficha Personal
Nombre: Laura Natalia Esquivel
Nacimiento: 18 de Mayo de 1994
Lugar: Buenos Aires (Argentina)
Signo zodiacal: Tauro
Familia: Su madre, Silvana, es ginecóloga, y su padre, Jorge, urólogo
Web: www.lauraesquivel.tv

Source: José Molina. "Laura Esquivel: Mucho más que un 'patito feo'," *OKAPI*, 98, October, 2010, p. 50. Reprinted with permission (text only) of Bayard-Revistas.

may not have, thereby creating an *information gap,* or a real need for students to provide and obtain information through the active negotiation of meaning (Shrum and Glisan, 2010; Waltz, 1996). Spontaneous conversation in the IPA requires a number of instructional strategies to help them develop communicative tactics. Some specific strategies that the teacher might use include:

- beginning with oral warm-up activities that lower the affective filter and provide students with thinking time;

- providing students with pre-thinking exercises or a graphic organizer to activate the thought process;

- providing students with video taped models of interpersonal communication and engaging them in analysis of the models;

- weaning students from using a written script or notes in their oral communication;

- providing multiple opportunities for student to practice "thinking on their feet" without the pressure of being evaluated constantly;

- providing students early on with conversational gambits in the target language as a means of negotiating meaning (e.g., *Could you repeat that please? Do you mean to say that…?);* a list of these expressions could be displayed in the classroom for part of the year until students are able to use them without reference to the list;

- including as a regular classroom feature opportunities to engage students in interpersonal communication on topics of school and individual interest, both with the teacher and with fellow classmates (e.g., opening of class when the teacher engages the class in sharing opinions about the upcoming basketball championship game);

- integrating ongoing opportunities for students to ask questions in the target language within tasks where there is an information gap, thus motivating students to make inquiries for real-world purposes;

- including activities in which students communicate with one another on some aspects of an interpretive task (e.g., an authentic reading or recorded segment);

- providing opportunities for each student to interact with a variety of peers, some of whom may have language proficiency below that of the student while others may have the same or higher proficiency; this ensures students will

at times assist students at a lower proficiency level while at other times they are challenged by students at their own or higher levels (Glisan et al., 2003, pp. 31-32).

Learning Activities to Prepare Students for the Presentational Task

In the presentational task students communicate a message to an audience of listeners, readers, or viewers. Since the audience is not usually able to negotiate meaning with the creator of the message, presentational communication is referred to as one-way communication. In the IPA students communicate messages by means of products that include oral public service announcements, short speeches, written essays or letters, and written articles. These products are often the culminating phase of the IPA and build upon the interpretive and interpersonal tasks.

The rubrics used to evaluate presentational communication include the use of the criterion called *impact*, which refers to the degree to which the message maintains the attention of the listener, reader, or viewer. The teacher should explore with students strategies for creating presentational products that have impact (e.g., selection of topic, use of visuals to support the message, choice of words, examples to engage the audience, or visual layout).

Preparing students to perform presentational tasks in the IPA requires a number of instructional strategies to help students produce messages that are clear and address the targeted audience. Some of those strategies include:

- beginning with warm-up activities that lower the affective filter and provide students with planning time;

- incorporating a process-oriented approach to presentational tasks with phases for drafting, peer editing, revising, and re-writing;

- offering feedback to students that includes attention to the message itself in addition to linguistic accuracy;

- providing periodic opportunities for students to judge the impact of the presentational messages of others so that they become more familiar with this aspect of their work;

- providing periodic opportunities for students to share their work with audiences other than the teacher and receive feedback from them;

• periodic videotaping of students' presentations and having students analyze their own work.

With implementation of the types of strategies outlined in this section, the teacher should find a seamless connection between classroom practice and the Integrated Performance Assessment.

References

Adair-Hauck, B., Glisan, E. W., Koda, K., Swender, E. B., & Sandrock, P. (2006). The Integrated Performance Assessment (IPA): Connecting assessment to instruction and learning. *Foreign Language Annals, 39*, 359-382.

Adair-Hauck, B. and Donato, R. (2010). PACE: Using a story-based approach to teach grammar. In J. Shrum and E. Glisan (Eds.) *Teacher's handbook: A contextualized approach to language instruction* 4th edition (pp.151-178). Boston, MA: Heinle Cengage Learning.

Adair-Hauck, B., & Troyan, F. J. (2013). A descriptive and co-constructive approach to Integrated Performance Assessment feedback. *Foreign Language Annals, 46*, 23-44.

Allen, E., Bernhardt, E. B., Berry, M. T., & Demel, M. (1988). Comprehension and text genre: An analysis of secondary foreign language readers. *The Modern Language Journal, 72*, 63–72.

Annenberg/Corporation for Public Broadcasting (CPB). (2004). *Teaching foreign languages K-12: Assessment strategies.* Retrieved from *http://www.learner.org/channel/libraries/tfl/assessment/index.html*

Black, P., & Wiliam, D. (1998). Inside the black box: Raising standards through classroom assessment. *Phi Delta Kappan, 80*(2), 139-148.

Byrnes, H. (2002). The role of task and task-based assessment in a content-oriented collegiate FL curriculum. *Language Testing, 19*, 419–437.

Davin, K. J., Troyan, F. J., Donato, R., & Hellmann, A. (2011a). Research on the Integrated Performance Assessment in an early foreign language learning program. *Foreign Language Annals, 44*, 605-625.

Davin, K., Troyan, F. J., Donato, R., & Hellmann, A. (2011b). A guide to IPA implementation in FLES Programs. *The Language Educator, 6*(4), 47-51.

Dristas, V. M., & Grisenti, G. (1995). Motivation: Does interest influence reading and speaking proficiency in second language acquisition? Unpublished manuscript.

Fredericks-Malone, C., & Gadbois, N. J. (2005/2006). Assessment, emotional scaffolding, and technology: Powerful allies in the K-12 world language classroom. *NECTFL Review, 57*, 21-29.

Galloway, V. (1998). Constructing cultural realities: "Facts" and frameworks of association. In J. Harper, M. Lively, & M. Williams (Eds.), *The coming of age of the profession* (pp. 129–140). Boston: Heinle & Heinle.

Glisan, E.W. (2010). Envisioning the big picture of program design. *The Language Educator, 5*(4), 7.

Glisan, E. W., Adair-Hauck, B., Koda, K., Sandrock, S. P., & Swender, E. (2003). *ACTFL Integrated Performance Assessment.* Yonkers, NY: ACTFL.

Glisan, E. W., Uribe, D., & Adair-Hauck, B. (2007). Research on Integrated Performance Assessment at the post-secondary level: Student performance across the modes of communication. *The Canadian Modern Language Review, 64*, 39-68.

Halverson, R., Pritchett, R. B., & Watson, J. G. (2007). *Formative feedback systems and the new instructional leadership* (WCER Working Paper No. 2007-3). Madison: University of Wisconsin–Madison, Wisconsin Center for Education Research. Retrieved from *http://www.wcer.wisc.edu/publications/workingPapers/papers.php*

Oguro, Y. (2008). *Presentation of culture in English-as-a-foreign-language reading textbooks in Japan.* Unpublished doctoral dissertation, Virginia Tech, Blacksburg, VA.

Sandrock, P. (2010). *The keys to assessing language performance. A teacher's manual for measuring student progress.* Alexandria, VA: ACTFL.

Shrum, J. L., & Glisan, E. W. (2010). *Teacher's handbook: Contextualized language instruction. 4th ed.* Boston, MA: Heinle Cengage Learning.

Supovitz, J. A., & Klein, V. (2003). *Mapping a course for improved student learning: How innovative schools systematically use student performance data to guide improvement.* Philadelphia: Consortium for Policy Research in Education, University of Pennsylvania.

Tharpe, R. G., & Gallimore, R. (1988). *Rousing minds to life: Teaching, learning, and schooling social contexts.* New York: Cambridge University Press.

Troyan, F. J. (2008). Being authentic: Assessing standards-based tasks in a content-based curriculum. *The Language Educator, 3*(4), 52-54.

Troyan, F. J., Davin, K., Donato, R., & Hellmann, A. (2012). Integrated Performance Assessment (IPA) in an elementary Sschool Spanish program. *Association for Childhood Education International Focus on the Elementary, 24*(3), 1-5.

Waltz, J. (1996). The classroom dynamics of information-gap activities. *Foreign Language Annals, 29,* 481-494.

Wiggins, G. (1998). *Educative assessment.* San Francisco: Jossey-Bass.

Wiggins, G., & McTighe, J. (2005). *Understanding by design* (expanded 2nd ed.). Alexandria, VA: Association for Supervision and Curriculum Development.

Young, D. J. (1999). Linguistic simplification of SL reading material: Effective instructional practice? *The Modern Language Journal, 83,* 350–366.

Chapter 5

Modeling and Feedback in the IPA

A primary goal of the educational standards movement in the United States during the 1990's was to transform assessment and learning from the traditional paradigm with embedded behaviorist learning theories to a new paradigm (Shepard, 2000). The assumptions embedded in behaviorism had the following consequences for teaching and testing:

- Learning occured by accumulating atomized bits of knowledge;
- Learning was tightly sequenced and hierarchical;
- Transfer was limited; each objective had to be explicitly taught;
- Tests were used frequently to ensure mastery before proceeding to the next objective;
- Tests were equated with learning (tests = learning);
- Motivation was external and based on reinforcement in many small steps (Shepard, 2000, p. 5).

The new paradigm is one in which assessment and instruction are integrated to enhance learning (Shepard, 2000; Shrum & Glisan, 2010). Learning is ultimately connected to rigorous standards (Hamilton, 2003; National Council on Education Standards and Testing, 1992) and the tests that assess them. In their description of assessment and learning in the new paradigm, called "the thinking curriculum," Resnick and Resnick (1992) remind us that (1) we get what we assess, (2) we don't get what we don't assess, and (3) we must design tests worth teaching to (p. 59). Wiggins (1998) echoes this tenet when he states, "Tests in their form and content teach students what kinds of adult challenges we value" (p. 21). The new paradigm, as outlined in the research on educational testing and accountability (Black & Wiliam, 1998; Resnick & Resnick, 1992; Shepard, 2000, 2003, Stiggins, Arter, Chappuis, & Chappuis, 2007), promotes a different role for assessment that is:

- part of a learning culture
- dynamic and ongoing
- a tool for evaluating prior knowledge

- an ongoing feedback cycle between students and teachers
- a vehicle for transfer of knowledge and skills
- a communicator of explicit criteria
- a means for student self-assessment
- an evaluative and self-reflective tool for teachers
- the locus of research.

The IPA is well situated within the new paradigm. Given the historical context and the role of feedback in a learning culture as described by Shepard (2000), we consider in this chapter the critical role of modeling and feedback in the IPA. In the first edition of this manual, the IPA was presented as a "cyclical approach" of "Modeling, Practicing, Performance, and Feedback phases" (Glisan, Adair-Hauck, Koda, Sandrock, & Swender, 2003; Wiggins, 1998) as Figure 5.1 depicts.

Figure 5.1 A Cyclical Approach to Second Language Learning and Development

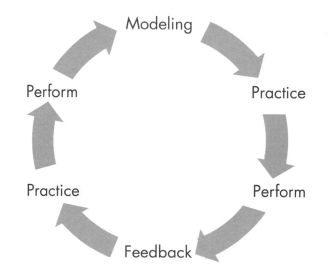

Source: Adapted from Wiggins, G., (1998).

In this publication, the critical role of modeling and feedback is illuminated through classroom examples of modeling, the discourse analysis of the Co-Constructive Approach (Adair Hauck & Troyan, 2013) to IPA feedback, and guidelines for teachers in providing this type of feedback. First, modeling in the IPA is presented and discussed from a social constructivist perspective. Second, the same theoretical approach is applied in the expanded description of the Co-Constructive Approach. Research describing the features of the discourse between the teacher and students in this approach to feedback is summarized. Third, based on those discursive features, characteristics of IPA feedback are outlined to assist teachers in providing descriptive and quality feedback on learner performance. Finally, those characteristics are applied to an example of the Co-Constructive Approach to actualize the characteristics of the feedback.

Modeling: Establishing Clear Learning Goals

The IPA framework of instruction and assessment assumes that performance is anchored to models of performance. Before students begin a unit of study, they view examples of the type of performance that is the goal of the instructional process (Adair-Hauck, Glisan, Koda, Swender, & Sandrock, 2006; Glisan et al, 2003; Hattie & Timperley, 2007; Sandrock, 2010; Shrum & Glisan, 2010; Wiggins, 1998; Wiggins & McTighe, 2005). Tharpe & Gallimore (1988) describe the importance of modeling as "a powerful means of assisting performance, one that continues its effectiveness into adult years and into the highest reaches of behavioral complexity" (p. 49).

An Example of Modeling in Instruction Linked to the IPA

When the IPA and associated instructional activities are planned according to the Understanding by Design (UbD) (Wiggins & McTighe, 2005) template described in Chapter Four, instruction can be linked to models, clear exemplars of performance that meet, exceed, or do not meet the standards. These models of performance facilitate the descriptive analysis of performance facilitated by rubrics (Glisan et al., 2003; Shrum & Glisan, 2010; Wiggins, 1998). Adair-Hauck and Troyan (2013) describe two types of modeling that occurred during a unit of instruction linked to the IPA.

The first type was at the beginning of the unit when students assessed interpersonal IPA tasks from the previous year. Using the Intermediate Interpersonal Rubric (see Appendix F), students rated videotaped performances and subsequently discussed the rating with the teacher. In their discussions, they referenced the specific domains or criteria (e.g., language function, text type, etc) on the rubric. This group rating process allowed the teachers and students to collectively identify the targeted performance before instruction began (Shrum & Glisan, 2010; Sandrock, 2010; Wiggins & McTighe, 2005).

The second type of modeling often occurred at the beginning of the class when the teacher and a student would model a speaking activity related to the theme. Once completed, the teacher and students group-rated the performance using the interpersonal rubric. Similarly, sometimes two students would perform or model an interpersonal speaking activity for the class, which was videotaped by the teacher and followed-up with group-rated feedback. The teacher's questions guided the group-rated feedback "Did they accomplish the task or purpose of the conversation?", "Was their language appropriately at the word, sentence or paragraph level?" "Did you see any negotiation of meaning?" etc.

Through modeling, the learners were able to "see" and to better comprehend the criteria of the interpersonal speaking rubric. After the modeling phase, the learners had time to practice through meaningful and theme-based interpersonal speaking activities. These interpersonal tasks involved teacher-to-student and student-to-student interaction in tasks that approximated the summative speaking task in the IPA. During the practice speaking activities, learners were able to make adjustments to try to improve their performance. Throughout the modeling and practicing phases, students were engaged in self-assessment, peer assessment, and co-constructive feedback discussions with the teacher using the IPA rubrics. This use of the IPA rubrics familiarized students with the rubric language, the types of performance associated with that language, and the procedures for the feedback that would occur during the summative IPA (Adair-Hauck & Troyan, 2013). In the following section, the Co-Constructive Approach to IPA Feedback is examined.

The Feedback Loop: Co-Constructing Performance Assessment Descriptions

In theoriginal IPA manual, Adair-Hauck (2003) presented the feedback loop as "responsive assistance" as the teacher guides a classroom of students through a feedback session related to their interpretive mode performance on the IPA. See Appendix I for a discussion of the differences between explicit or co-constructive (responsive) feedback for the interpretive mode.

In this publication, the discussion of the feedback loop has been expanded to account for feedback on interpersonal tasks (Adair-Hauck & Troyan, 2013). From a social constructivist perspective, the "feeding-back" (Tharp & Gallimore, 1988) of information related to performance is a process that occurs between the individual as expert (e.g., the teacher, a parent, some other mentor) through guided participation (Rogoff, 1990, 2003) in communities of practice (Duff, 2003; Gutiérrez, Buquesdano-López, & Alvarez, 1999; Hattie & Timperley, 2007; Lave, & Wenger, 1991; Rogoff, 1994). Contrary to traditional forms of teacher-student feedback—which have traditionally been tests, scores, and other marked papers—a social constructivist perspective views feedback as dialogic interaction in which the expert (the teacher) and the apprentice (the student) co-construct a performance assessment (Adair-Hauck & Troyan, 2013). Many scholars have advocated such a constructivist approach to feedback in assessment that involves the student more closely in the assessment process (Muñoz & Alvarez, 2010; Shepard, 2000, 2003; Tunstall & Gipps, 1996, Wiggins, 2005). Pryor and Torrance (2000) point out that assessment is not something that teachers do *to* learners; rather, they posit that it is:

> *accomplished by means of social interaction in which the practices of the participants have a critical effect on the outcome. The outcomes of assessment are actively produced rather than revealed and displayed by the assessment process. Moreover, each participant brings to the event understandings not only of the cognitive agenda, but also of the kind of social relations and practices that are legitimate in the circumstances (p. 126).*

The co-construction of a performance assessment description between the teacher and student is the essence of the feedback loop of the IPA. A community of practice (Lave & Wenger, 1991) for feedback is developed over time through the mentoring of questioning techniques and other discourse strategies. This section presents the Co-constructive Approach to IPA feedback (Adair-Hauck, 2000, 2003; Adair-Hauck & Troyan, 2013; Troyan and Adair-Hauck, 2011). To contextualize the discussion, research is reviewed to establish the critical role of feedback in assessment and learning.

"The Power of Feedback"

Research has offered insight into the types of feedback that may be the most effective for improving student performance. Hattie and Timperley (2007) found feedback to be in the top 5 of 10 factors impacting achievement in the studies that they analyzed. Beyond identifying "The Power of Feedback," it was found that the effect of feedback on performance varied by type: *task feedback* showed the highest effect sizes whereas praise, rewards, and punishment had lower effect sizes associated with them. *The most effective types of feedback offer assistance (e.g., cues, reinforcement), utilize technology (video, audio, computer) in feedback delivery, and connect to goals.* Kluger and DeNisi (1996) went well beyond the realm of feedback in the classroom. In their synthesis of feedback studies in work, school, and other performance situations, the authors concluded that feedback is a highly complex process that is context-dependent. The authors derive several practical suggestions from their analysis. Feedback is most effective when it features:

- tasks that are familiar to students and connect to standards and analogous tasks
- cues that support future learning
- a focus on the task and not the student
- consistency in feedback practices (Kluger & DeNisi, 1996).

These studies provide an overall picture of the impact of feedback on learning using statistical analyses. Furthermore, they reinforce the critical role of modeling and feedback in the IPA. However, understanding the complexity of feedback as a social practice requires qualitative research approaches.

The Discourse of Feedback

To unpack the discursive nature of a co-constructive feedback, it is important to qualitatively describe the interaction between teacher and student. Building on Sadler's (1989) paper, which outlines the ways in which teachers might use feedback to articulate the standards to be achieved and move students toward "evaluative expertise" (p. 143), Tunstall and Gipps (1996) describe a typology of feedback based on their qualitative study of 49 children in years 1 and 2 and 8 teachers across 6 London schools. Through the analysis, four types of feedback were identified along a continuum from evaluative to descriptive (called Types A, B, C and D). Moving across the continuum, the evaluative types are A1: Rewarding; A2: Punishing; B1: Approving; B2: Disapproving. The descriptive types are C1 Specifying attainment; C2: Specifying improvement; D1: Constructing achievement; and D2: Constructing the way forward.

Types C and D are the most salient for the current discussion, as they correspond to the standards-based and social constructivist model of feedback advocated for IPA feedback (Adair-Hauck, 2003). To simplify this typology for the IPA feedback loop, Types C and D have been renamed Type 1 and Type 2, respectively and are depicted in the continuum in Figure 5.2 below.

Figure 5.2 Continuum of Feedback Types in the IPA Feedback Loop

Type 1   **Type 2**

Monologic   Dialogic
Teacher-Directed   Student-Led

In Type 1, the student is provided with models for desired performance, and improvements are suggested based on those models. This is the moment when the teacher can articulate a clear performance goal and secure the student's commitment to achievement (Kluger & DeNisi, 1996, p. 260) by communicating the standards (Sadler, 1989) during modeling activities (Wiggins, 1998). Type 1 is monologic (usually teacher to student), however, and does not allow for student participation, whereas type 2 engages students and empowers them in the process of identifying "aspects of competence" that emerge in their work (Tunstall & Gipps, 1996, p. 399) through a co-constructed description of performance (Adair-Hauck & Troyan, 2013). Type 1 exchanges

may be more characteristic of early conversations when performance standards and/or the feedback process are new to the novice student. As they complete tasks and become more familiar with the descriptors, students can begin to identify gaps in their own performance, moving gradually toward Type 2 exchanges, the goal in the Co-Constructive Approach to IPA feedback.

The Role of Questions in a Co-constructive Approach
Questioning is at the core of co-constructive feedback. Tharp and Gallimore (1988) identified two types of questions: assessing and assisting. Assessing questions determine the level at which the student can perform without assistance, whereas assisting questions support the student to reach a level of performance that he or she could not reach unassisted. Teachers can use assessing questions to determine the appropriate level of instruction, or to move into the student's zone of proximal development (ZPD), "the distance between the learner's actual developmental level as determined by independent problem-solving (unassisted performance) and the level of potential development as determined through problem-solving under adult guidance (assisted performance)" (Vygotsky, 1978). Assessing questions, although they provide the teacher with vital information for instruction, serve a limited role, as they do not assist learning. Assisting questions, on the other hand, function within the student's ZPD, where the student can generate that which he cannot or is unwilling to construct alone (Tharpe & Gallimore, 1988). Although both types of questions serve a role, assisting questions are the predominant type in the IPA feedback model articulated here.

Adair-Hauck and Troyan (2013) describe the features of co-constructive IPA feedback regarding interpersonal mode performance. The three tasks of the intermediate-level IPA completed by the high school students are summarized in Table 5.1. The IPA was administered at the end of a unit exploring famous persons of the Francophone world. The study presents a discourse analysis of an IPA interpersonal task feedback session between the teacher and a student who *meets expectations* on the Intermediate Interpersonal Rubric. In summary, the exchange between the student and the teacher featured:

1. dialogic and bi-directional feedback *mediated and negotiated by the expert and apprentice through language;*

2. ample assisting questions and cognitive probes to help the learner to self-assess, self-reflect, and self-regulate;

3. discourse mirroring everyday language used outside of instructional settings.

Table 5.1 Famous Persons of the Francophone World Intermediate Level—IPA Task Overviews

Interpretive
Your teacher will give you a reading dealing with the life of a famous person from the Francophone world. Your job is to understand as much as you can from this reading so that you can discover the kind of information you may want to use for your letter of nomination for naming your school's French club. Take up to 20 minutes to read and show your understanding of the article.

Interpersonal
You and your partner have to decide the name of the French Club. Based on the research that you have conducted on a famous person over the past weeks, you will now talk to your partner and decide for which of your two people the club will be named. Decide on one of the two and give good reasons for the choice that you make.

Presentational
Based on information you have read as well as your discussion with your classmate, write a letter of nomination of approximately 200 words (three paragraphs) for naming your school's language club chapter after a famous person from the Francophone cultures. Briefly describe the person's personal life and professional accomplishments. Write about why the person is popular in his/her own country and also in the US. Be sure to make the case why you want to name your club after this person. Remember you are writing to members of your language club. Take up to 40 minutes to prepare your letter of nomination.

Based on the analysis of the interaction, Adair-Hauck and Troyan (2013) summarized the discourse features and the characteristics of the Co-Constructive Approach to IPA feedback. Table 5.2 serves as an outline of the major discourse patterns observed in the interaction. Table 5.3 provides a summary of the characteristics of co-constructive feedback to guide teachers in implementing this type of feedback in their classrooms.

Table 5.2 Discourse Features used to Facilitate a Co-Constructive Approach to IPA Feedback

1. Dialogic or symmetrical combination of teacher and student talk
2. Judicious use of explicit directives and metastatements; mainly used initially to define task and establish a context.
3. Use of first person collective pronouns "we" for joint-problem solving
4. Sparse use of assessment questions
5. Abundance of assisting questions and cognitive probes
6. Use of presuppositions, ellipsis and abbreviated speech (mirroring everyday language)
7. Language, especially questions, needs to be attuned to a level where performance requires assistance

Source: Adair-Hauck & Troyan (2013)

Table 5.3 Characteristics of a Descriptive and Co-Constructive Approach to IPA Feedback

1. Focus on learner performance compared to model performance
2. Language development is a work in progress
3. Questioning as part of the discussion
4. Mutual appraisal of performance is integral to descriptors
5. Shifting responsibility of learner's own role in learning/assessing
6. Brainstorming of strategies to improve performance
7. Active participation of learner to self-assess and self-regulate
8. Reflective process for both teacher and learners
9. Lack of evaluative or judgmental statements

Source: Adair-Hauck & Troyan (2013)

Exploring Discourse Features of Co-Constructive IPA Feedback

In this section, the discourse between a teacher and a student engaged in IPA feedback is presented. The study was conducted during the 2008–2009 academic year in a combined level 3-4-5 French class with 20 students at a public urban high school in the northeastern United States. Language classes met for 90-minute blocks every other day all year. Language study was organized around long-term units of inquiry. The IPA became the locus around which instruction, feedback and reflective systems for language learning were designed. Ongoing student reflection toward meeting course standards occurred in all classes in the school, thus the feedback loop that is part of the IPA was congruent with the culture of modeling, practicing, performing, continuing feedback and reflecting on standards-based performance at school.

The goals of this section are twofold. First, it provides an additional example of the Co-Constructive Approach to IPA feedback for the interpersonal mode. Second, it features the assessment of two students; one rated as *meets expectations* and one rated *does not meet expectations* on the Intermediate interpersonal rubric. Collectively, these exemplars serve as models for teachers implementing this approach to feedback.

The sample IPA feedback occurred after the student had performed the videotaped interpersonal Famous Person task with a partner.

- First, the student viewed her performance from the videotape;
- Second, the teacher and student assessed her performance individually;
- Third, the teacher and student co-construct IPA feedback.

This process for interpersonal assessment is aligned with Kluger and DeNisi's (1996) research on feedback which underscores that the most effective types of feedback offer assistance (e.g. cues, reinforcement), use technology (video, audio, computer) in feedback delivery, and connect to goals.

The discourse examined in Figure 5.3 is from the IPA feedback session for the Famous Person IPA depicted in Table 5.1. At the time of the study, this student was in 10th grade and had been studying French for 4 years. The "Famous Person" IPA was her third IPA. In the IPA feedback protocol below, key discursive features outlined in Tables 5.2 and 5.3 are highlighted to illuminate the nature of the Co-Constructive Approach (Adair-Hauck & Troyan, 2013).

The Co-Constructive Approach to IPA feedback depicted in Figure 5.3 has many of the characteristics underscored by Adair-Hauck and Troyan (2013) from their study (See Table 5.2). First, the focus of the IPA feedback session is to compare the student performance to model performance, not to some other student's performance or to a set of statistical norms. The rubric explains to both the teacher and the student the criteria to judge the performance as well as the range in quality of the performance. Second, a lack of judgmental statements, such as "Good"; "Great"; or "Well done", is evident in the feedback session. The teacher, using the rubric as a language learning "tool", provides rich and descriptive feedback that highlights what the student *can do* with the language in spontaneous, unscripted discourse. Third, since a major goal of the teacher is to encourage the student to self-assess, he uses assisting questions to encourage the student to self-reflect, self-assess and reflect on her language performance. Through language and co-constructive feedback, the teacher empowers the student by shifting the responsibility of the IPA assessment.

The protocol is an interesting example of how learners are "apprentices in thinking" (Rogoff's term, 1990). At first, the student underrates her interpersonal language performance; she rates herself as *weak meets* for both Language Function and Text Type. The teacher (expert) gives the student the latitude to rate herself first. In this way, she is able to share her thoughts without any predispositions. After the learner shares her self-assessment, the teacher provides his appraisal and explains *why* she has underrated herself in two critical domains for Intermediate interpersonal speaking (Language Function and Text Type). However, Lindsay is not that far off in her self-assessment because she rates herself at the "meets" level for Intermediate interpersonal speaking. In a sense, she is just a "sub-level" off for each of these two domains. In many ways, the discourse highlights that Lindsay is moving towards evaluative expertise. That is, she is assuming more control over her own performance and the assessment of that performance. In the process, she is gaining a clearer sense of exactly where she is on the "continuum of performance." Her language awareness and metacognition are clearly facilitated by this co-constructive approach. The above discourse highlights how co-constructive IPA feedback encourages mutual appraisal of performance, and

Figure 5.3 Co-Constructive IPA Feedback Session: Meets Expectations
Feedback Loop Example 1 — Lindsay

Lindsay completed the interpersonal task with Ashlie, the student featured in the Adair-Hauck and Troyan (2013) study.

Part 1: Lindsay assesses her overall *task completion*

T: So in the end, you decided on your person. So that gets to my question: ***Did you complete the task that was asked of you?***

| | Assessment question to define the task. |

S: I think so.

T: Okay. And how so?

| | Assisting question probing student to explain "why". |

S: Because we picked a person…and there was a reason why.

T: How do you in English just recap what that reason was?

S: It was because um we thought that my person was like a better role model for um people, especially like young girls because she is like a real person, like relatable whereas like she wasn't you know, kind crazy with being a celebrity or anything, whereas Ashlie's person was kind of, you know, very, kind of fake and not a very good person, so…

| | Student defends why she thinks she completed task. |

T: Let's start with the top part, ***Language Function.***

| | "Let's" denotes joint problem solving. |

S: Um… I said that I created in a basic way or created language in a basic way because I felt like I didn't I wasn't necessarily expressing all that I could expressing all that I could express or what I wanted to so I thought it was just kind of basic. It wasn't extraordinary or whatever. Um… for ***Text Type, I said simple sentences and some strings of sentences.*** A lot of times, I was just kind of explaining little bits and pieces. I wasn't necessarily explaining the whole picture all at once. So yeah… that's why I picked that. Umm…the next one [***Communication Strategies***] is kind of the same thing, I guess.

| | Learner self-reflecting & self-assessing |

T: yeah?

| | Teacher's rising intonation asking for more information. |

S: By asking and answering questions, both Ashlie and I like would ask clarifying questions if we needed to or so it was the same.

T: What kind of clarifying questions did you ask?

S: Well, there was a verb that she used that was like "to act" like the actual verb "acting". And I didn't know what that meant and I had to clarify what that was and she had to negotiate the meaning of that. And she also had to ask me a couple of questions about what I was talking about just like the movie or whatever she was saying.

| | Learner reflects on how she negotiated meaning by questioning. |

T: When you had to, you were able to clarify for meaning, right?

| | Assisting question to encourage learner to reflect on her ability to ask questions. |

S: yeah…so that was good. And then…

| | Learner responds and evaluates her performance. |

Figure 5.3 (cont.) Co-Constructive IPA Feedback Session: Meets Expectations
Feedback Loop Example 1 — Lindsay

T: Did you ever clarify by paraphrasing, using different words?

Assisting question regarding use of paraphrases as a communication strategy.

S: Ahhh…no. I don't think so. I don't really know. There wasn't a bit time where I had to do that. I was more like just answering questions she had…so…

Learner explains she didn't need to paraphrase.

T: Okay. Okay.

S: Um…and I thought I was generally understood by those **accustomed with the interaction with language learners because I mean Ashlie is also a language learner and**… she understood me or whatever, so….That was that. Um….I thought I was on the weaker side of the meets section for language control because I was able to like, do little…make little sentences…but it wasn't necessarily like a full thing. So, it was mostly just kind of like simple sentences….nothing big.

Learner reflects on her comprehensibility.

T: And…What did we miss here?

S: Nothing.

T: How was your…were you mainly working in the present tense? Past tense?

Assisting question asking learner to reflect on her use of present/past tense.

S: Uh…I did both. Because I talked about how when she was younger, like how she *became* an actress and how she wanted to sing but um she got into acting because of her parents. And then I talked about presently, she's in the movie *La Vie en Rose* and kind of that presently, she's a good role model.

Learner's reflection on tense use.

T: So, just to come back up here [**points to the top of the Rubric:** *Language Function and Text Type* **where the student had rated herself as** *weak meets.*], I think you're a little hard on yourself here. And it is true that you are working with someone who is [makes a gesture indicating that her speaking partner was a higher level than her]…so working with Holly [Lindsay's partner in the mid-year IPA] at one end and working with Ashlie at the other end…um…you handled yourself well. You could tell you were nervous working with her, just because of your body language, but you still, you're still working in the **strong meets** um…things where maybe that there just weren't opportunities to clarify by paraphrasing…but you definitely clarified by asking questions …and uh…that's clear. Umm…and I mean…definitely understood by someone *accustomed to working with language learners,* if not beyond that. So, I think you…you're selling yourself a little short there. Um…but um…it's just important for you to know that you can survive in those newer situations where you're speaking with someone who is more advanced. You're going to encounter that in France when you go there soon. So…okay?

Teacher's offers his assessment compared to learner's self-assessment and explains why the learner needs to adjust her rating.

Teacher compares learner's performance to past performance.

Authentic use of language in IPA related to real-world use of language.

S: Mmm Hmm.

T: Anything else that you wanted to mention?

S: No

T: Thank you.

therefore, it can be a reflective process for both the teacher and the learner. (See Appendix J for sample IPA feedback for a learner who does not meet expectations.)

Improving Student Performance through IPA Assessment and Feedback

Some teachers may be concerned with the issue of time for co-constructive IPA feedback. However, as more teachers explore IPA assessment, various approaches to feedback are being applied in different instructional contexts. For example, some teachers prefer to co-construct IPA feedback with pairs of students. Other teachers have reported that once students are familiar with the rubric descriptors, co-constructive IPA peer assessment can be an effective means to assist learners to think about their language performance. In other words, through modeling and frequent dialogic teacher-to-student or student-to-student IPA feedback, students become effective self and peer assessors (Adair-Hauck, 2011).

In another study, Troyan and Adair-Hauck (2009) highlight that IPA assessment, which includes modeling, practice, performance, and co-constructive feedback, leads to improved learner performance. The study of 15 students in a high school French curricular program grounded in IPAs depicts the effect of instruction linked to the IPA on student performance. Before IPA assessment, students in this study had great difficulty speaking interpersonally. In fact, the students themselves demanded more explicit focus on the interpersonal mode of communication. They indicated that they did not feel equipped to handle the demands of spontaneous speaking. As a result, the teacher restructured learning activities (See Chapter 4) to be congruent with the IPA. All 15 of the students in the study improved their interpersonal speaking performance after participating in three IPAs. Note also, that for this IPA research project, the researchers integrated Hattie and Timperly's (2007) recommendations that the most effective feedback focuses on task feedback, offers assistance (hints, cues, reinforcement) and utilizes technology.

Two students did not initially meet the standard. These students were assisted through co-constructed feedback to focus on strategies and plans that would lead them to meet the standard in a subsequent IPA interpersonal speaking task (See Appendix J). This approach is in keeping with Wiggins (1998) who stresses that learners need opportunities to review, revise and resubmit work for evaluation against the standard. The findings of the study underscore the benefits of IPA assessment, which in this study included co-constructed IPA feedback. Students who were not able to communicate interpersonally before the study were able to meet the standard for interpersonal communication by the end of the study because of their participation in IPA, which includes the four major constructs: modeling, practicing, performing and co-constructive feedback (Troyan & Adair-Hauck, 2009).

In conclusion, Hattie and Timperly's (2007) seminal article on the power of feedback, suggests three questions to guide learners as they try to meet the goals of the standards:

"Where am I going?"
"How am I going?
"Where to next?"

It should be noted that after this feedback session, the teacher encouraged the learner to think about how she was going to improve her language performance, i.e., feedback constructing the way forward or "Where to next?" (Hattie and Timperly, 2007). Using these three guiding questions, Adair-Hauck and Troyan (Adair-Hauck & Troyan, 2013; Troyan & Adair-Hauck, 2011) suggest the following guidelines presented in Table 5.4 for co-constructive IPA feedback.

Table 5.4 Teachers and Learners as Co-Constructors of IPA Feedback

1. To set the learners up for success, ensure that they are familiar with the IPA rubrics. Providing models of student performance across the modes will enable them to better understand the question, "Where am I going?" or "What are the goals?"

2. During the feedback loop, both the teacher and learner review language performance (via audio or video if interpersonal or presentational speaking), then individually they assess the performance using the IPA rubric. Allowing the learner the opportunity to self-assess first will shift more of the responsibility onto the learner. When the student is not sure how to assess his/her performance, is confused, bewildered etc., the teacher's assisting questions may help the learner to better understand and assess his / her performance. After the learner's appraisal, the teacher matches his/her rating with the student. Most importantly, teacher and learner should assess and acknowledge why the performance is at a particular level, i.e., "How am I going?"

3. Through the use of the teacher's critical assisting questions or cognitive probes, co-constructive IPA feedback shifts or places the responsibility on the student to appraise and assess his/her performance.

4. Cognitive probes will also prompt and support the learners to perceive, observe and examine their work, that is to think about their progress in language learning.

5. The teacher and students together discuss strategies that will help to improve performance and plan for future achievement/performance, or "Where to Next?"

6. Co-constructive IPA feedback allows for both teacher and students to be learners in the IPA assessment/ learning process.

Source: (Adair-Hauck & Troyan, 2013; Troyan & Adair-Hauck, 2011)

References

Adair-Hauck, B. (2000). *Exploring a socially-constructed feedback approach to Integrated Performance Assessment.* Paper presented at the University of Pittsburgh. Pittsburgh: PA.

Adair-Hauck, B. (2003). Providing responsive assistance using the IPA feedback loop. In Glisan, Adair-Hauck, Koda, Sandrock, & Swender, *The ACTFL Integrated Performance Manual* (pp.11–15). Yonkers, NY:ACTFL.

Adair-Hauck, B., Glisan, E. W., Koda, K., Swender, E. B., & Sandrock, P. (2006). The Integrated Performance Assessment (IPA): Connecting assessment to instruction and learning. *Foreign Language Annals*, 39, 359–382.

Adair-Hauck, B. (2011). *The IPA Feedback Loop: Assisting questions that foster self- assessment, self-reflection and self-regulation.* Presentation for the New Jersey Department of Education (Title VI grant). Trenton: New Jersey.

Adair-Hauck, B. & Troyan, F. J. (2011). *The IPA Feedback Loop: Keys to Improving L2 Learner Performance.* Paper presented at the Northeast Conference on the Teaching of Foreign Languages, Baltimore, Maryland.

Adair-Hauck, B., & Troyan, F. J. (2013). A descriptive and co-constructive approach to Integrated Performance Assessment feedback. *Foreign Language Annals*, 46, 23–44.

Black, P., & Wiliam, D. (1998). Inside the black box: Raising standards through classroom assessment. *Phi Delta Kappan*, 80(2), 139–148.

Duff, P. (2003). Intertextuality and hybrid discourses: The infusion of pop culture in educational discourse. *Linguistics and Education*, 14, 231–276.

Glisan, E. W., Adair-Hauck, B., Koda, K., Sandrock, S. P., & Swender, E. (2003). *ACTFL Integrated Performance Assessment.* Yonkers, NY: ACTFL.

Gutiérrez, K., Buquesdano-López, P., & Alvarez, C. (1999). Building a culture of collaboration through hybrid language practices. *Theory into Practice*, 38(2), 87–93.

Hamilton, L. (2003). Assessment as a policy tool. *Review of Research in Education*, 27, 25–68.

Resnick, L. B., & Resnick, D. P. (1992). Assessing the thinking curriculum: new tools for educational reform. In B. R. Gifford & M. C. O'Connor (Eds.), *Changing assessment: Alternative views of aptitude, achievement, and instruction* (pp. 37–75). Boston: Kluwer.

Hattie, J., & Timperley, H. (2007). The power of feedback. *Review of Educational Research*, 77, 81–112.

Kluger, A. N., & DeNisi, A. (1996). The effects of feedback interventions on performance: A historical review, a meta-analysis, and a preliminary feedback intervention theory. *Psychological Bulletin*, 119, 254–284.

Lave, J. & Wenger, E. (1991). *Situated learning: Legitimate peripheral participation*. New York: Cambridge University Press.

Muñoz, A. P., & Álvarez, M. E. (2010). Washback of an oral assessment system in the EFL classroom. *Language Testing*, 27, 33–49.

National Council on Education Standards and Testing. (1992). *Raising standards for American education*. Washington, DC: Author. Retrieved from http://www.eric.ed.gov:80/PDFS/ED338721.pdf.

Pryor, J., & Torrance, H. (2000). Questioning the three bears: The social construction of classroom assessment. In A. Filer (Ed.), *Assessment: Social practice and social product* (pp. 110–128). Oxford: Routledge.

Resnick, L. B., & Resnick, D. P. (1992). Assessing the thinking curriculum: New tools for educational reform. In B. R. Gifford & M. C. O'Connor (Eds.), *Changing assessment: Alternative views of aptitude, achievement, and instruction* (pp. 37–75). Boston: Kluwer.

Rogoff, B. (1990). *Apprenticeship in learning*. Oxford: Oxford University Press.

Rogoff, B. (1994). Developing understanding of the idea of communities of learning. *Mind, Culture, and Activity, 1*, 209–229.

Rogoff, B. (2003). *The cultural nature of human development*. Oxford: Oxford University Press.

Sadler, D. R. (1989). Formative assessment and the design of instructional systems. *Instructional Science*, 18, 199–144.

Sandrock, P. (2010). *The keys to assessing language performance: A teacher's manual for measuring student progress*. ACTFL: Alexandria, VA.

Shepard, L. A. (2000). The role of assessment in a learning culture. *Educational Researcher*, 29(7), 4–14.

Shepard, L. A. (2003). Reconsidering large-scale assessment to heighten its relevance to learning. In J. M. Atkin & J. E. Coffey (Eds.), *Everyday assessment in the science classroom: Science educators' essay collection* (pp. 121–146). Arlington, VA: National Science Teachers Association Press.

Shrum, J. L., & Glisan, E. W. (2010). *Teacher's handbook: Contextualized language instruction* (4th ed.). Boston, MA: Heinle Cengage Learning.

Stiggins, R., Arter, J., Chappuis, J., & Chappuis, S. (2007). *Classroom assessment for student learning: Doing it right—using it well*. Upper Saddle River, NJ: Pearson Prentice Hall.

Tharpe, R. G., & Gallimore, R. (1988). *Rousing minds to life: Teaching, learning, and schooling social contexts*. New York: Cambridge University Press.

Troyan, F. J., & Adair-Hauck, B. (2009). [Investigating the effect of the integrated performance assessment on instruction and student learning]. Unpublished raw data.

Troyan, F. J., & Adair-Hauck, B. (2011). *The Integrated Performance Assessment and Feedback Loop: Keys to Improving L2 Performance.* Paper presented at the Northeast Conference on the Teaching of Foreign Languages, Baltimore, MD.

Tunstall, P., & Gipps, C. (1996). Teacher feedback to young children in formative assessment: a typology. *British Educational Research Journal*, 22, 389–404.

Vygotsky, L. (1978). *Mind in society.* Cambridge, MA: Harvard University Press.

Wiggins, G. (1998). *Educative assessment.* San Francisco: Jossey-Bass.

Wiggins, G. (2005). More feedback on real tasks: Less evaluation based on audits only. Retrieved from http://www.grantwiggins.org/documents/E&H.pdf

Wiggins, G., & McTighe, J. (2005). *Understanding by design.* Alexandria, VA: Association for Supervision and Curriculum Development.

Chapter 6

Examples of IPAs from the Field

This chapter presents a collection of IPAs from instructors in K–12 and university settings. Representing a range of languages, these IPAs are meant to serve as exemplars for the field. It is important to note that, although they are presented here as models, these IPAs were created for specific instructional contexts. Therefore, the exact texts, tasks, and content may not be applicable in all classrooms. Our intention is that these IPAs will serve as inspiration for other teachers in the design and implementation of their own IPAs.

The IPA is situated as a key classroom-based assessment providing evidence of learners' improvement in using language for specific communicative purposes as well as evidence of progressing along the literacy continuum detailed in the Common Core State Standards (ACTFL, 2012; National Governors Association Center for Best Practices [CCSSO], 2010). Given the goals articulated in these standards and based on literacy research, the interpretive mode task and rubric have been redesigned to view literacy as a developmental process rather than a skill that develops according to strictly defined levels. Interpretive tasks at all levels provide students with opportunities to demonstrate literal and interpretive comprehension. As explained in Chapter 2, given the background knowledge of learners, their age, and their prior experience with text interpretation, the specific type of tasks and texts may vary. For example, inferencing for a third grader might consist of anticipating what will happen next in a story, while for an adult learner it might consist of gleaning the author's viewpoint on an abstract topic through the text. Furthermore, the format used for the inferencing task may be tailored to the level of the learner, as indicated in the template that appears in Appendix D. Ideally, all elements on the interpretive guide would be covered in the interpretive task, particularly so that learners have an opportunity to show whether or not they can "exceed expectations" on the rubric. If teachers find that designing interpretive tasks that incorporate all the elements in the template for a selective text to be particularly challenging (such as, organizational features, comparing cultural perspectives, or personal reactions, etc.), the teachers may want to reconsider the text for the IPA task. Culturally-rich, multi-dimensional and engaging texts will naturally lend themselves to these thought-provoking interpretive tasks. In this way, IPA assessment provides learners with cognitively-challenging tasks to "exceed expectations" on the rubric, and tangentially, demonstrates to school administrators how the curriculum is aligned with the Common Core State Standards' (CCSSO, 2010) view of literacy development. (For more information, see the discussion in Chapter 4 regarding text selection.)

The IPA examples presented in this chapter move from units targeting the novice level through the intermediate level to the intermediate high and advanced levels. The language educators who designed the IPAs have used them in their classes and provide the overview and details on all three tasks. Following the Understanding by Design model, the language educators teach their unit of instruction with the summative IPA assessment tasks clearly in mind, preparing students with the knowledge and skills and with sufficient practice to be successful on the tasks. By keeping the IPA performance tasks in mind, the teacher covers and develops background knowledge during the unit of instruction, as well as practices the strategies the learners will need to use in the assessment, for example, addressing text interpretation through instructional activities that develop students' ability to "grapple" with texts "to become college and career ready" (CCSSO, 2010. p. 35).

Sample Integrated Performance Assessments

Novice
Vacations (Spanish, High School)
International Studies (Spanish, University)

Intermediate
Famous Persons (Spanish, High School)
Ecology (French, High School)
Poetry as Social Commentary (Latin, High School)

Intermediate High
Healthy Eating (Spanish, High School)
Immigration (Spanish, University)
Dandelion School Transformation Project (Chinese, High School)

Advanced
Divorce (Spanish, University)
Freedom (Arabic, University)

SPANISH, NOVICE LEVEL
Theme: **Vacations**

Instructor: José Pan, Edison School District, New Jersey
Standards Addressed:
Interpersonal Communication
Interpretive Communication
Presentational Communication
Relating Cultural Practices to Perspectives
Making Connections
Cultural Comparisons

Task Overview

In this unit, you will go on a virtual vacation to Madrid, Spain to learn about its attractions, food, and culture. In the first part of the unit before the IPA interpretive piece you will learn about different places and attractions to visit in Madrid. You will learn information about the metro to help you use it before the interpretive assessment. For the interpretive task, you will read a web page that highlights the Madrid metro system and the advantages of using it to move around the city. The interpersonal assessment involves a role play where you are trying to get from one place to the next by asking a ticket agent (a classmate) directions as well as pertinent information in order to reach your ultimate destination. The final part of the unit focuses on visiting several websites such as museums and restaurants to do some sightseeing and take in what Madrid has to offer. For the presentational task, you will write a letter to your pen pal in Chile to tell him about the fun things to do in Madrid. You also decide that you will send him some pictures of the interesting attractions such as museums and restaurants that one can visit in Madrid.

Interpretive Task

You are on vacation with your family in Madrid. You all decide to head out and go sightseeing but no one is sure what the best way to travel throughout the city is. You head downstairs to the hotel lobby and sign on to the Internet to see what would be good means of transportation. Your web search leads you to the following web page. Read the page and then answer the following questions in English as best as you can.

Interpersonal Task

Your family has decided to go see a museum today, but you are not really in a museum type of mood. You and your older brother decide on going to the movie theater instead to see the cool movie you see advertised everywhere. In the hotel lobby you are informed that the closest theatre around is at "SOL" and that you'll need to take the subway. You head to the "Serrano" subway station, right across the street from your hotel. At the ticket booth you meet the friendliest vendor in the world. While asking him for directions on how to get from your station to Sol he realizes you are a visitor and strikes up a conversation asking you questions about yourself and where you are from. Answer his questions, but do not forget to ask him for directions on how to get to the movie, because after all you do not want to spend all day in a subway station talking to a stranger about every aspect of your life. You have a movie to catch! Materials Needed: Madrid subway map from the Internet

Presentational Task

Your vacation in Madrid now comes to a close and you are on the way back to the United States. The flight back is long and there is nothing interesting to listen to on the in-flight channels. The movie on the plane is not interesting and you are bored out of your mind. So you reach into your carry-on bag and pull out pictures you took while in Madrid. You realize how much fun you had and a thought enters your mind. You decide you want to write a letter to your pen pal, Javier Pazos, in Chile to tell him about the fun things to do in Madrid. You also decide that you will send him some pictures you took of the museums and restaurants you visited while there. You pull out your laptop and create your letter to Javier.

Interpretive Phase: *Las vacaciones*

Materials Needed: Pre-reading activity, web page, comprehension questions, rubric, pen or pencil.

Teacher Notes:

1. Students should answer the pre-reading questions in pairs. (15 mins.)

2. Students then read the Internet article and answer the accompanying comprehension questions individually. (25 mins.)

Pre-reading Activity for Interpretive IPA Tasks
Read the following questions and think about how you would answer them. Once you are done, share your answers with a partner.

1. Where is Madrid located?

2. What is the monetary currency in Spain? What did it replace?

3. What other information do you know about Madrid or Spain in general?

4. What types of transportation have you been on? Which one do you prefer?

Special Needs Adaptations:

1. Have the words from section I of the task highlighted for the students.

2. Read the passage once aloud for students as they follow along on their paper. Students then read the passage before answering the questions.

Novice Level Interpretive Task Comprehension Guide: Las Vacaciones: WEBMADRID
http://www.webmadrid.com/guia/transporte/metro.asp

NOMBRE: _____ FECHA:_____

I. Key word recognition.
Find in the article the Spanish word that best expresses the meaning of the following English words.

a. transportation _____

b. ticket booth _____

c. entrances _____

d. complicated _____

e. direction _____

f. hallway _____

g. cabins _____

h. information_____

i. service _____

j. station _____

II. Main idea:

Using information from the article, describe in English the main purpose of the webpage.

_____

_____

_____

III. Supporting details.

For each of the following,

- Circle the letter of each detail that is mentioned in the article (not all are included!)
- Write the letter of that idea next to where it appears in the text.
- Write the information that is given in the article in the space provided next to the detail below.

A. The fastest means of transportation in Madrid. _____

B. The place where one can purchase a metro ticket. _____

C. The metro line where musicians like to play. _____

D. How the metro lines are marked to help you find your way. _____

E. The price of a one way ticket. _____

F. The price per ticket for senior citizens to ride the metro. _____

G. How first class metro cars are marked. _____

H. The hours the subway is open. _____

IV. Organizational features. How is the text organized? Choose all that apply and explain briefly why you selected each organizational feature—what were the clues in the text?

A. Chronological
B. Pros and Cons
C. Cause and effect
D. Compare and Contrast
E. Informational

Justification from text:

_____

_____

_____

V. Guessing Meaning from Context. Based on this passage write what the following three words/phrases probably mean in English.

1. **DESPLAZARSE EN** (1st paragraph) _____

2. ¿Quieres ver el **PLANO**? (3rd paragraph) _____

3. "**ES BASTANTE SENCILLO**" (5th paragraph) _____

VI. Inferences: "Read between the lines" to answer the following questions, using information from the text. Your responses should be in English.

1. Why do you think that the author states, "Las líneas del Metro de Madrid crecen casi cada año y disponemos ya de una de las mejores redes de toda Europa"?

_____

_____

2. Why do you think that it is important for American students to have an understanding of Madrid's metro before traveling to this famous city? Use information from the text to support your ideas.

_____

_____

VII. Author's Perspective. Select the perspective or point of view you think the author adopted as s/he wrote this article and justify your answer with information from the text. Respond in English.

A. Comic
B. Moral
C. Informative

Justification from text:_____

_____

VIII. Comparing Cultural Perspectives. Answer the following questions in English:
1. How does the Madrid Metro train system compare to a train/subway system that you know?

_____

_____

_____

2. Would this article have been different if it were written for a U.S. audience? Why or why not?

_____

_____

_____

IX. Personal Reaction to the Text. Using specific information from the text, describe your personal reaction to the article in **Spanish**. Be sure to provide reasons/details that support your reaction.

IPA Las vacaciones —
Assessing the Presentational Mode

Materials Needed: computers with Internet access, writing assignment and graphic organizer, rubric, pen or pencil.

Teacher Notes: Two class periods should be spent on research. Try to have these two classes where students can use computers to access the Internet to get the photos and info they need for the writing assignment. Students should also bring their rough drafts one day before they are due so they could have their papers peer edited and checked for mistakes.

Pre-writing

Students are to think about the following questions before they begin this task.

1. What are some things you might be able to see in Madrid?

2. Where might you be able to get something to eat in Madrid?

3. Where might you be able to do some shopping?

Special Needs Adaptation: A graphic organizer is provided to help students outline their letters.

NOMBRE: _____   FECHA:_____

Presentational Task

STUDENT PROMPT: Your vacation in Madrid now comes to a close and you are on the way back to the United States. The flight back is long and there is nothing interesting to hear on the radio. The movie on the plane is not interesting and you are bored out of your mind. So you reach into your carry on bag and pull out pictures you took while in Madrid. You realize how much fun you had and a thought enters your mind. You decide you want to write a letter to your pen pal, Javier Pazos, in Chile to tell him about some of the fun activities to do in Madrid. Your letter should be typed and include the following information:

1. A formal greeting explaining how you love Madrid.

2. Suggestion of one or two hotels where he could stay.

3. A famous museum and where he could see two paintings that you love.

4. Your thoughts on the paintings.

5. A restaurant where the food is great with a suggestion for a memorable meal, how much it cost and your opinion of it. (imagine)

6. How you can get around in Madrid. (transportation)

7. Your overall opinion about Madrid

8. A farewell

Graphic Organizer

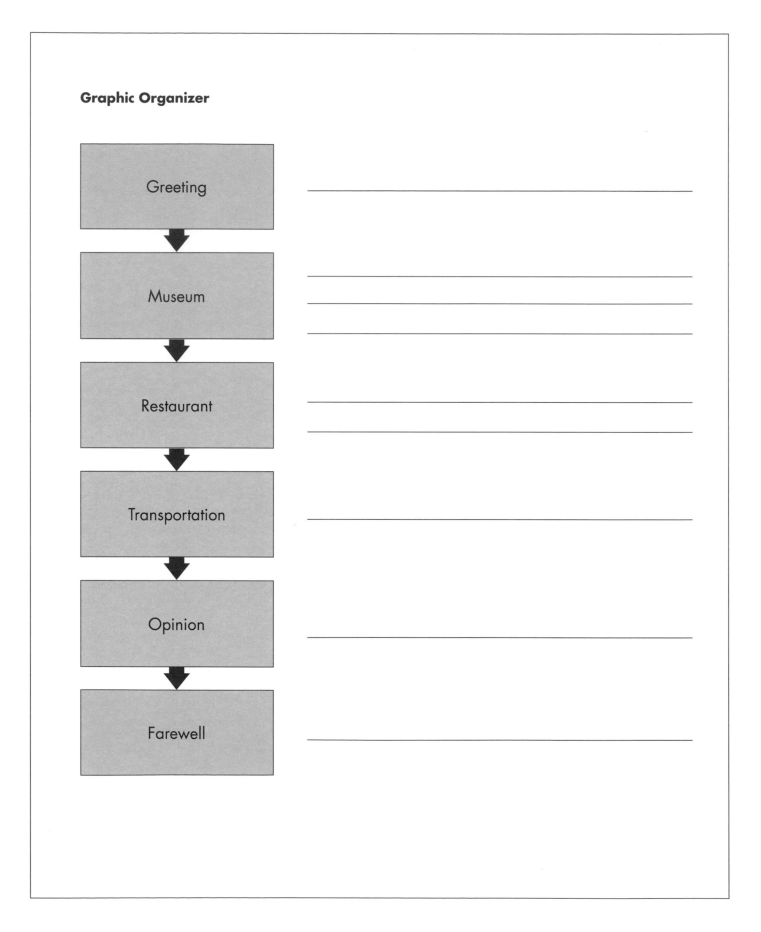

SPANISH, NOVICE LEVEL
Theme: **International Studies**

Drs. Mandy Menke, Grand Valley State University
Cynthia Korsmo, Grand Valley State University
Standards Addressed:
Interpersonal Communication
Interpretive Communication
Presentational Communication
Relating Cultural Practices to Perspectives
Relating Cultural Products to Perspectives
Acquiring Information
Cultural Comparisons

Task Overview

The university will be traveling to various study abroad fairs in Spanish-speaking countries. You have been assigned the responsibility of creating a flier to promote GVSU to prospective international studies interested in studying in the U.S. In order to create this brochure, you first gather some information about what universities are like in Spanish-speaking countries. Then you will discuss with a classmate aspects of your life at the university. Finally, you will create a flier for GVSU.

Interpretive Task

In order to understand what international universities are like, you look for information on the Internet. Your teacher finds the following text about *la Universidad de Puerto Rico en Río Piedras*. Read the text carefully and complete the comprehension questions that accompany it. Note to teacher:

Interpersonal Task

Now that you have information about a university in a Spanish-speaking country, you need to gather more information about the university experience of other students at GVSU. Talk with a classmate to learn more about his/her personal activities at the university. You want to know about his/her majors, classes, daily schedule, living situation, weekend/leisure activities, and transportation. Find out as much as you can from your partner in order to incorporate some of the details into your flier.

Presentational Task

Based on what you have learned from your research, your knowledge of the university, and class discussions, create a flier in which you promote GVSU to Spanish-speaking university students. Your flier might include information about classes, living situations, transportation, recreational opportunities (sports/clubs/other campus/regional activities).

Recintos | Río Piedras
Universidad de Puerto Rico en Río Piedras

El Recinto de Río Piedras de la Universidad de Puerto Rico ofrece sobre 80 programas de bachillerato, más de 55 maestrías y sobre 14 programas doctorales.

A esto se le añade, la Escuela de Derecho (que ofrece Juris Doctor y Maestría en Derecho), certificados post bachillerato, certificado post maestría, y programas de educación continua.

Con una población estudiantil de aproximadamente 17,624, la UPRRP es la es la unidad con más estudiantes y posee los programas graduados y profesionales de maestría y doctorado más abarcadores del Caribe.

Es la universidad líder en investigación en Puerto Rico y cuenta con un sistema de 29 bibliotecas muchas de ellas, especializadas en temas particulares.
Su amplia oferta académica proviene de las siguientes escuelas y facultades:
- Facultad de Estudios Generales
- Facultad de Administración de Empresas
- Escuela de Arquitectura
- Facultad de Ciencias Naturales
- Facultad de Ciencias Sociales
- Escuela de Derecho
- Facultad de Educación
- Facultad de Humanidades
- Escuela de Comunicación
- Escuela Graduada de Ciencias y Tecnologías de la Información
- Escuela Graduada de Planificación

Cada facultad y escuela ofrece una variedad programas de práctica profesional, intercambio con universidades extranjeras, proyectos de investigación y otras ofertas para el desarrollo profesional del estudiante.

La UPRRP es considerado el corazón de la zona comercial y cultural de Río Piedras, ubicada en la región central de la cuidad capital de San Juan. Es fácilmente accesible a través de transportación pública, incluyendo el Tren Urbano que llega hasta las inmediaciones del recinto que es fácilmente identificado a la distancia por su emblemática torre.

El recinto combina veredas, y áreas verdes entre edificios antiguos y modernos que sirven de evidencia del desarrollo arquitectónico de los pasados 105 años en la arquitectura puertorriqueña.

La vida universitaria en Río Piedras es vibrante y muy dinámica. El recinto cuenta con un Museo, Teatro, Estación de Radio, Periódico impreso y Digital, múltiples facilidades deportivas, centros de investigación y sobre 50 organizaciones estudiantiles reconocidas entre las que destacan por su reconocimiento internacional el Coro de la Universidad, La Tuna de la Universidad y el Teatro Rodante.

El Recinto de Río Piedras de la Universidad de Puerto Rico. http://www.upr.edu/?type=page&id=recintos_RioPiedras&ancla=RioPiedras. Reprinted with permission by University of Puerto Rico, Committee of Intellectual Property.

Spanish: Novice Level Interpretive Task Comprehension Guide: International Studies
"La Universidad de Puerto Rico en Río Piedras"

I. Key Word Recognition. Find in the article the Spanish word/phrase that best expresses the meaning of each of the following English words/phrases:

1. University choir _____

2. old buildings _____

3. Department / College _____

4. professional internships / practice _____

5. green spaces _____

6. research _____

7. sports facilities _____

8. Master's (degree) _____

9. Doctoral programs _____

10. Bachelor (degree) _____

II. Main Idea. Using information from the article, provide the main idea of the article in English.

_____

_____

_____

III. Supporting Details.
Circle the letter of each detail that is mentioned in the article (not all are included!).
Write the letter of the detail next to where it appears in the text.
Write the information that is given in the article in the space provided next to the detail below.

Location of the University: _____

Campus dining: _____

Architectural style of buildings: _____

Class demands: _____

Extracurricular activities: _____

Opportunities to work on campus: _____

Ways of arriving on campus: _____

Student life: _____

IV. Organizational Features.
How is this text organized? Choose all that apply and explain briefly why you selected each organizational feature--what were the clues in the text?

A. Alphabetical order
B. Description
C. Compare/contrast
D. Pros and cons
E. Problem and solution

Justification from text: _____

V. Guessing Meaning From Context. Based on this passage, write what the following three words/phrases probably mean in English:

1. **reconocimiento** internacional (last paragraph) : _____

2. el **desarrollo** profesional (5th paragraph); el **desarrollo** arquitectónico (7th paragraph): _____

3. **intercambio** con universidades extranjeras (5th paragraph):_____

VI. Inferences. "Read between the lines" to answer the following questions, using information from the article. You may respond in Spanish or English.

1. Would students enjoy time with friends outside of class on this campus? Be sure to use details from the article to support your answer.

_____

_____

_____

2. Why do you think students choose to study at this campus?

_____

_____

_____

VII. Author's perspective. Select the perspective or point of view you think the author adopted as s/he wrote this article and justify your answer with information from the text. You may respond in Spanish or English.

A. Clinical/scientific
B. Informative
C. Historical

Justification from text:_____
_____
_____

VIII. Comparing Cultural Perspectives. Answer the following questions in Spanish or English:

1.Compared to typical descriptions of universities in the US, what does this college not appear to have?

_____
_____

2. What are some physical features of the campus that are similar to GVSU?

_____
_____
_____

Describe how the presence or lack of these features (from #1 and #2) affect or portray the values held by the students, the faculty/staff, and the culture as a whole?

_____
_____
_____

IX. Personal Reaction to the Text. Using specific information from the text, describe your personal reaction to the article **in Spanish**. Be sure to provide reasons that support your reaction.

Some phrases to help you get started:
(No) me gusta… porque..
Deseo … porque…
Prefiero …. porque…

SPANISH, INTERMEDIATE LEVEL
Theme: **Famous Persons**

Dr. Eileen Glisan, Indiana University of Pennsylvania
Standards Addressed:
Interpersonal Communication
Interpretive Communication
Presentational Communication
Relating Cultural Practices to Perspectives
Relating Cultural Products to Perspectives
Cultural Comparisons

Task Overview

You are a member of the language club at school. The club members have decided to name the club in honor of a famous person from the Spanish/Hispanic culture. All members will vote soon in order to select a famous person in whose honor the club will be named. However, you all need to do some research in order to make a good decision! After locating some interesting descriptions of famous people from the Spanish-speaking world, you decide to read an article about Laura Esquivel, a famous actress, which has recently appeared in the popular magazine *Okapi*. After reading the article, you discuss this famous person as a possible candidate with a classmate, as well as discussing the classmate's choice from the article s/he has read. Finally, you make a decision and write a letter of nomination for the famous person of your choice. Your letter must be convincing to the other members of the language club.

Interpretive

Your teacher will give you a reading dealing with the life of a famous person from the Spanish-speaking world. Your job is to understand as much as you can from this reading so that you can discover the kind of information you may want to use for your letter of nomination for naming your school's Spanish club. Take up to 20 minutes to read and show your understanding of the article.

Interpersonal

You and your partner have to decide the name of the Spanish Club. Based on the research that you have conducted on a famous person over the past weeks, you will now talk to your partner and decide on which of your two people the club will be named after. Decide on one of the two and give good reasons for the choice that you make.

Presentational

Based on information you have read as well as your discussion with your classmate, write a letter of nomination of approximately 200 words (three paragraphs) for naming your school's language club chapter after a famous person from the Spanish-speaking world. Briefly describe the person's personal life and professional accomplishments. Write about why the person is popular in his/her own country and also in the US. Be sure to make the case of why you want to name your club after this person. Remember you are writing to members of your language club. Take up to 40 minutes to prepare your letter of nomination.

Spanish: Intermediate Level Interpretive Task Comprehension Guide: Famous Person

(See Chapter 4 p. 35 for authentic document for Laura Esquivel)

I. Key Word Recognition. Find in the article the Spanish word/phrase that best expresses the meaning of each of the following English words/phrases:

1. "Ugly Ducking": _____

2. singer: _____

3. stage design: _____

4. to get on stage: _____

5. career: _____

6. children's comedy: _____

7. show (noun): _____

8. opened for the first time (movie): _____

9. soap opera: _____

10. stages (noun; as in growing up): _____

II. Main Idea. Using information from the article, provide the main idea of the article in English.

_____
_____
_____

III. Supporting Details.
- Circle the letter of each detail that is mentioned in the article (not all are included!).
- Write the letter of the detail next to where it appears in the text.
- Write the information that is given in the article in the space provided next to the detail below.

A. Four areas that Laura Esquivel began to study when she was 7 years old:

_____

B. What her grandfather Horacio Esquivel had to say about Laura:

_____

C. The professions of her parents:

_____

D. What Laura said about receiving the news that she got the part in "Patito feo":

_____

E. Place and date of Laura's birth:

_____

F. How Laura spends her leisure time with friends:

_____

G. Laura's successes beyond "Patito feo":

_____

H. Laura's hopes for dating and marriage:

_____

IV. Organizational Features. How is this text organized? Choose all that apply and explain briefly why you selected each organizational feature—what were the clues in the text?
A. Chronological order
B. Pros and cons
C. Compare/contrast
D. Biography/Autobiography
E. Problem and solution

Justification from text:_____

V. Guessing Meaning From Context. Based on this passage, write what the following three words/phrases probably mean in English:

1. algo de ese espíritu artístico lo había **heredado** de su abuelo (1st paragraph): _____

2. su gran oportunidad de **triunfar** internacionalmente (3rd paragraph): _____

3. Aunque ha estado **de gira** con su espectáculo Patito feo (4th paragraph): _____

VI. Inferences. "Read between the lines" to answer the following questions, using information from the article. Your responses may be in English or in Spanish.

1. What personal attributes does Laura Esquivel have that have contributed to her success? Explain.

_____

_____

_____

_____

2. How does Laura feel about playing roles in productions geared to adults? Use details from the article to support your answer.

_____

_____

_____

VII. Author's perspective. Select the perspective or point of view you think the author adopted as he wrote this article and justify your answer with information from the text.
A. Comic
B. Factual
C. Moral/Religious

Justification from text:_____

VIII. Comparing Cultural Perspectives. Answer the following questions in Spanish:

1. Re-read the note in the lower right-hand corner of the text that begins "Ha dicho..." Relate this note to practices and perspectives of the Hispanic culture.

_____

_____

_____

2. What similarities and differences might there be between this article and an article that were written about a person from the U.S.?

_____

_____

_____

IX. Personal Reaction to the Text. Using specific information from the text, describe your personal reaction to the article **in Spanish**. Be sure to provide reasons that support your reaction.

FRENCH, INTERMEDIATE LEVEL
Theme: Ecology

Istructor: Tara Aucoin, Mahwah Public Schools, New Jersey
Standards Addressed:
Interpersonal Communication
Interpretive Communication
Presentational Communication
Relating Cultural Practices to Perspectives
Relating Cultural Products to Perspectives
School and Community

Task Overview

What changes can we make in our daily lives to help protect our environment?

In your French class, you have been studying some of the problems facing our environment and exploring the effect of these problems on people all over the word. To help promote individual responsibility when it comes to protecting the environment, you are going to make a slide-show presentation for the students at the Collège Condorcet, your partner school in France, in which you describe steps that they and students everywhere can take to protect our planet. First you will read an excerpt of an article from a French adolescent magazine promoting environmentally friendly practices to give you some ideas. Then, you will discuss with a partner the positive or negative impact on the environment of different practices at your school. Finally, you will create a presentation for the students at the Collège Condorcet explaining some of the practices that they could adopt in efforts to better protect the environment.

Interpretive

After learning about the dangers facing our environment, you want to know what you can do to help make a difference. To help you get started, you will consult an excerpt from the article "L'écolo dico rigolo," (Bayard Presse). Read the excerpt carefully and complete the accompanying comprehension activity.

Interpersonal

With your partner, try to identify all the things your school is currently doing to help the environment and come to agreement on any habits that pose a risk for the environment. See if you can agree on what practices help and which practices harm the environment and why or how.

Presentational

Based on the information your conversation provided, you are going to recommend a few steps that students in your partner school can take to help protect our planet. You will make a slide-show presentation for your pen-pal, describing an environmental concern that you studied in class and the different ways your partner school can help by altering students' daily routines.

Mathieu Rocher. "L'écolo dico rigolo," *ASTRAPI*, 770, April 2012, p.2-7. Illustrations, Marion Puech. Graphics, Lorraine Harris.
Reprinted by permission of Bayard Presse.

French Intermediate Level Interpretive Task Comprehension Guide: Ecology

I. Key Word Recognition. Find in the article the French word/phrase that best expresses the meaning of each of the following English words/phrases:

1. trash can: _____

2. garbage: _____

3. fresh: _____

4. instead of: _____

5. disturb: _____

6. to pick up: _____

7. leave (as in exit): _____

8. a snack: _____

9. wrapped: _____

10. to turn on (something): _____

II. Main Idea. Using information from the article, provide the main idea of the article in English.

_____

_____

_____

III. Supporting Details.
- Circle the letter of each detail that is mentioned in the article (not all are included!).
- Write the letter of the detail next to where it appears in the text.
- Write the information that is given in the article in the space provided next to the detail below.

A. What dressing warm in cold weather prevents:

_____

B. Two ways you can respect the environment when going on walks in nature:

_____

C. Why halogen lamps are not environmentally friendly:

_____

D. How to properly dispose of broken lamps:

_____

E. The amount of trash the country of France disposes of each year:

_____

F. Ways you can promote environmental responsibility at school:

_____

G. Why it is better to pack and eat snacks from home:

_____

H. The impact the internet has on the environment:

_____

IV. Organizational Features. How is this text organized? Choose all that apply and explain briefly why you selected each organizational feature—what were the clues in the text?

A. Alphabetical order
B. Letter/message
C. Compare/contrast
D. Pros and cons
E. Dos and Don'ts

Justification from text: _____

V. Guessing Meaning From Context. Based on this passage, write what the following three words/phrases probably mean in English:

1. une **ampoule** basse consommation (1st paragraph) : _____

2. le pays le plus **éloigné** de France (4th paragraph) : _____

3. un réflexe **malin** (5th paragraph) : _____

VI. Inferences. "Read between the lines" to answer the following questions, using information from the article. You may respond in French or English.

1. Why is it important that you buy fruit when it is in season? Be sure to use details from the article to support your answer.

2. Why does this article mention walking as one way to help the environment?

VII. Author's perspective. Select the perspective or point of view you think the author adopted as he wrote this article and justify your answer with information from the text. You may respond in French or English.

A. Clinical/scientific
B. Humanistic
C. Educational

Justification from text: _____

VIII. Comparing Cultural Perspectives. Answer the following questions in French or English:

1. What do the suggestions mentioned in this article reveal about French cultural perspectives?

2. Based on the article, what are some cultural similarities and/or differences between France and the United States?

IX. Personal Reaction to the Text. Using specific information from the text, describe your personal reaction to the article in **French**. Be sure to provide reasons that support your reaction.

[Possible additional question to elicit personal reaction]

In your opinion, which recommendation is the most realistic for you as a high school student to follow? Which recommendation is the least realistic? Why?

LATIN, INTERMEDIATE LEVEL
Theme: **Poetry as Social Commentary**

Tracy Seiler, South Carolina Virtual School Program
Standards Addressed:
Interpersonal Communication
Interpretive Communication
Presentational Communication
Relating Cultural Practices to Perspectives
Cultural Comparisons

Overview to the Integrated Performance Assessment:
In this unit, you will read authentic, unadapted poems
of Martial to discover how poetry can be used to delve
into the political, social, economic and cultural mores
of the Roman people and compare these mores to those
of modern American society.

Unit Essential Questions

- How can poetry better express certain ideas than
other genres?
- How does the flexibility of the Latin language aid the
composition of poetry?
- What do the poems of Martial and Catullus reveal
about Roman social and cultural values?
- In what ways do the poems of Martial and Catullus
differ from the type of poetry written by Americans
and in what ways are they similar?

Interpersonal Task

You use your Twitter account to tweet your response in Latin
about two poems of Martial. Read and respond to two posts
from other students, agreeing or disagreeing and explaining why. Ask questions about the person's comments or to
clarify what was said.

Interpretive Task

Complete an interpretive task comprehension guide for the
two poems given. Analyze the text for information about
Roman culture and relate this information to what you have
learned.

Presentational Task

Create your own two-line poems in Latin using elegiac cou-
plets, to tell a joke or make an observation about a person
(who will be referred to only by a pseudonym). Read your
poem aloud on VoiceThread and other students will com-
ment on the poem in Latin, either orally or in writing.

Latin IPA: Martial Poems for Interpretive Task

1.23
Invitas nullum nisi cum quo, Cotta, lavaris
et dant convivam balnea sola tibi.
Mirabar quare numquam me, Cotta, vocasses*:
iam scio me nudum displicuisse tibi*.

*voca[vi]sses
*scio me displicuisse tibi...
  I know that I have displeased you

1.91
Cum tua non edas, carpis mea carmina, Laeli.
Carpere vel* noli nostra vel* ede tua.

*vel...vel: either...or

Latin Interpretive Task Comprehension Guide
Intermediate Level
Stage 29: Martial, Poems 1.23 and 1.91

I. Key Word Recognition: List the words/phrases/clauses from the poems that best express the meaning of each of the following English words/phrases/clauses and give their line numbers:

1. unless: _____

2. give: _____

3. when I am naked: _____

4. publish: _____

5. you take: _____

6. our poems: _____

7. alone: _____

II. Main Idea: Using information from the reading, outline the main plot of these poems in English. One or two sentences should be sufficient. Do NOT translate the poems!

_____

_____

_____

III. Supporting Detail
- Circle the letter of each detail that is mentioned in the poems (not all are included!).
- Write the letter of the detail next to where it appears in the poem.
- Write the information that is given in the poems in the space provided next to the questions below.

Write your response in English.

A. What Cotta is fond of? _____

B. Where does Cotta invite Martial? _____

C. What does Cotta think of Martial's personality?_____

D. What does Cotta think of Martial's appearance? _____

E. What does Laelius publish?_____

F. What does Laelius like to eat? _____

G. What is the reason for Cotta's party? _____

IV. Meaning from Context:

Based on the passage, write what the following words most likely mean in English and give one English derivative (a word that comes from the Latin word) for each.

1. nullum (poem 1.23): _____

2. mirabar (poem 1.23): _____

3. scio (poem 1.23): _____

4. ede (poem 1.91): _____

V. Inferences:

Answer the following questions by supplying as many reasons or as much information as you can. Your responses may be in English or Latin.

1. How does Martial suggest that Cotta is shallow in poem 1.23?

_____

_____

2. What do you think Martial emphasizes most in poem 1.23 and why?

_____

_____

VI. Cultural Perspectives

How would a modern American poet deal with someone ripping off their work?

SPANISH, INTERMEDIATE HIGH LEVEL
Theme: **Healthy Eating**

Instructor: Dr. Michele Schreiner,
Egg Harbor Township Public Schools
Standards Addressed:
Interpersonal Communication
Interpretive Communication
Presentational Communication
Relating Cultural Practices to Perspectives
Making Connections
Cultural Comparisons
School and Community

Task Overview

In just a few short weeks you will begin your *au pair* job for this summer (a household assistant working for and living as part of a host family with young children in a Spanish-speaking country). You've recently been in contact with the family that you'll be working with and the mother has told you she wants your assistance to help get her three children on a healthy diet this summer. To prepare yourself for this task you decide to do some reading on healthy foods parents should feed their children. You and a friend talk about how to handle situations when children don't want to eat vegetables. Finally, you create a book to send to the family to demonstrate that you know a lot about healthy eating.

Interpretive

To help you prepare for your job as an *au pair* you need to do some reading. You're going to be working for a family with three children, ages 2, 7 and 12. In addition to entertaining them this summer, you will also be cooking for them and you've been instructed to get them on healthy diets. Read the article about foods parents should feed to their children and answer the questions.

Read the article and complete the accompanying "Comprehension Guide." [Note: The article from Sesame Workshop is no longer available from their website.]

Interpersonal

Since you will be spending all day everyday this summer with the children and feeding them, their parents are concerned with healthy eating. Share with a friend a story about a time when you or someone in your family didn't want to eat vegetables; explain what your parent did and discuss similarities and differences about how such issues were handled in your home and that of your conversation partner. (N.B. Students do not read any written notes during the interpersonal task. The interpersonal task is a spontaneous two-way interaction.)

Presentational

You really want to do a good job as an au pair this summer so you decide to go all out and learn as much as you can about nutrition and healthy eating so that you'll be ready when you step off the plane. Write and illustrate a children's book that encourages healthy eating by comparing bad vs. good eating habits. Children often like animals or other young children; so you may want to choose an animal or cartoon character who had bad eating habits (you'll need to use the past tense); and now has good eating habits; and how this change has made a great difference in his/her life. Be prepared to read your story for the 4th and 5th graders who are learning Spanish as practice for reading it to the family you'll be working for.

Spanish: Intermediate High Interpretive Comprehension Guide: Healthy Eating
Plaza Sésamo: ¿Qué comen los niños?

I. Key Word Recognition. Find in the article the word/phrase in the target language that best expresses the meaning of each of the following English words:

1. to nourish oneself _____

2. fats _____

3. beans _____

4. reduce _____

5. suggests _____

6. nutritious _____

7. will remain _____

8. to choose _____

9. improve _____

10. to taste _____

II. Main Ideas. Using the information from the article, write *2–3 complete sentences* in English to explain the main idea.

_____

_____

_____

III. Supporting Details. Based on the article, which of the following statements are discussed in the article?
- Circle the idea on the *answer sheet* (NOT ALL APPEAR!!!)
- Write the letter of the detail next to where it appears in the text.
- Briefly share or summarize the information given in the article on your answer sheet under the appropriate number. (DO NOT COPY THE ENTIRE PARAGRAPH!!!)
- If the statement is not discussed in the article, do not mark the idea; leave it blank.

1. The kinds of fruits and vegetables one should eat daily.

   _____

2. Most Mexican children's diets contain too much of this.

   _____

3. When you become an adult your diet should include more of this.

   _____

4. Aside from eating healthy, children should do this at school.

   _____

5. Mexican children should eat this rather than processed foods.

   _____

6. Specific times of the day you should not eat a lot of grains.

   _____

7. At the dinner table, it's a good idea to mix food with this.

_____

8. The name of the chemical pesticide found in processed food that can be dangerous for children's health.

_____

IV. Organizational Features. How is this text organized? Choose all that apply and explain briefly why you selected each organizational feature—what were the clues in the text?

A. Chronological
B. Pros and cons
C. Cause/effect
D. Problem/solution
E. Biography

Justification from text: _____

V. Guessing Meaning from Context.
Based upon this article, write what the following phrases mean in English (they are circled in the article so they can be found easily):

(p.2 a la izquierda) **aconseja** Dr. Mendoza: _____

(p.2 a la izquierda)…**carece de** _____

(p.2 a la derecha) … **proporcionan** un gran contenido de nutrimentos _____

VI. Inferences: "Read between the lines" to answer the following questions using information from the text. Your responses should be in Spanish.

1. Based on what you read in the article, why do you think the author includes the section at the end with tips? Please explain in 2-3 complete sentences in Spanish.

_____

_____

_____

2. Based on what you read in the article, what might be the effect if mothers continue to give their children processed foods? Please explain in 2-3 complete sentences in Spanish.

_____

_____

_____

VII. Author's Perspective. Select the perspective or point of view you think the author adopted as he/she wrote this article and justify your answer with information from the text.

1. Historical
2. Comic
3. Factual

Justification from Text: _____

VIII. Comparing Cultural Perspectives.

Answer the following question in Spanish:
If the author had been writing this article for a U.S. audience, what might the similarities and differences be?

_____

_____

_____

Personal Reaction to the Text: (Note to teachers: this section should not be graded)
Using specific information from the text, describe your personal reaction to the article in **Spanish**. Be sure to provide reasons for your reaction. Connect to your own experiences or to other things you have read, learned, or seen about the topic (from other classes or outside of school).

Theme: **Immigration**

US Air Force Academy
Eileen W. Glisan, Daniel Uribe and Bonnie Adair-Hauck*
Standards Addressed:
Interpersonal Communication
Interpretive Communication
Presentational Communication
Relating Cultural Practices to Perspectives
Making Connections
Cultural Comparisons

*Note: This IPA, which focuses on listening/viewing in the interpretive mode, was designed using the Interpretive Task Comprehension Guide published in the *ACTFL Integrated Performance Assessment Manual (1st* edition), 2003. The post-secondary IPA was published in an article by Glisan, E., Uribe, D., and B. Adair-Hauck (2007). The Integrated Performance Assessment: Evaluating student performance across the three modes of communication. *Canadian Modern Language Review* special volume on language assessment, 64(1), 39–67. Research project conducted at the U.S. Air Force Academy.

Interpretive

Instructions: We have been studying the theme of immigration for the past two weeks. After watching the video clip from "Espejo Enterrado," answer the questions below. You will watch the video twice. Recommended strategy: answer the questions in section II as you watch the video the first time, then answer the rest of the questions after you've watched the video a second time. ¡Buena Suerte!

Interpersonal

During this portion of the Integrated Performance Assessment, you will be debating the issue of illegal immigration into the US. You will be asked to either defend an "open door" policy on illegal immigration as presented by Carlos Fuentes, or argue against it. Use the information you learned in part I of the assessment (interpretive mode) and also the information you have learned about this topic throughout the course to defend your position. Your discussion will be recorded and graded using the rubric you have been provided.

Presentational

For the next lesson, write a paper (1–2 pages) describing your opinion about illegal immigration into the US. Use the information you learned from Part I of the IPA (Interpretive mode) and also information from your discussion/debate to support your point of view. You will also do a 2–3 minute oral presentation on the same topic. You are allowed to have one note card if you need it.

**Integrated Performance Assessment, Intermediate-High
(Note that this IPA was originally labeled "Pre-Advanced")**

Part I
Interpretive Mode

Instructions: After watching the video clip from "Espejo Enterrado," answer the questions below. You will watch the video twice. Recommended strategy: answer the questions in section II as you watch the video the first time, then answer the rest of the questions after you've watched the video a second time. ¡Buena Suerte!

I. Idea Principal *[Main Idea]*
Write a short (2–3 sentences) summary of the video passage IN ENGLISH.

_____

_____

_____

II. Detalles Importantes. Responda a las siguientes preguntas EN ESPAÑOL. *[Important Details. Respond to the following questions in Spanish.]*

1. La frontera entre los EEUU y México es la única frontera visible entre _____ y _____.
[The border between the U.S. and Mexico is the only border visible between _____ and _____.]

2. Algunos dicen que la frontera no es una frontera sino una _____ .
[Some say that the border isn't a border, but rather a _____.]

3. De acuerdo al Sr. Fuentes, ¿cuál es la ventaja que tienen los inmigrantes ilegales en contra de la patrulla fronteriza?
[According to Mr. Fuentes, what advantage do the illegal immigrants have over the border patrol?]

_____

4. ¿Qué pasa con los inmigrantes ilegales cuando son capturados?
[What happens to the illegal immigrants when they are captured?]

_____

5. ¿De que se acusa a los inmigrantes ilegales en los EEUU? Mencione por lo menos dos cosas.
[What are the illegal immigrants accused of in the U.S.? Mention at least two things.]

_____

6. ¿Por qué siguen cruzando los inmigrantes ilegales a los EEUU?
[Why do illegal immigrants continue crossing the border to the U.S.?]

_____

III. Implicaciones. Responda a las siguientes preguntas EN ESPAÑOL. *[**Implications.** Respond to the following questions in Spanish.]*

1. ¿Qué quiere decir el Sr. Fuentes cuando dice que "…es difícil llegar al otro lado"?

[What does Mr. Fuentes mean when he says that "it is difficult to reach the other side"?]

_____

_____

_____

2. ¿Qué quiere decir el Sr. Fuentes cuando dice "y sólo más tarde llegaron los anglo-americanos"?

[What does Mr. Fuentes mean when he says "and only later did the Anglo-Americans arrive"?]

_____

_____

_____

IV. Perspectivas del Autor. Responda a las siguientes preguntas EN ESPAÑOL.

*[**Author's perspectives.** Respond to the following questions in Spanish.]*

1. El Sr. Fuentes pregunta: "¿No será ésta siempre una tierra hispánica?" ¿Qué implica el Sr. Fuentes con esta pregunta?

[Mr. Fuentes asks, "Will it not always be a Hispanic land? What does he imply by this question?]

_____

_____

_____

2. ¿Qué solución propondría el Sr. Fuentes al problema de inmigración ilegal a los EEUU?

[What solution would Mr. Fuentes propose to the problem of illegal immigrant to the U.S.?]

_____

_____

_____

V. Reacción Personal. Responda a la siguiente pregunta EN ESPAÑOL. *[**Personal reaction.** Respond to the following questions in Spanish.]*

¿Qué opina usted del punto de vista del Sr. Fuentes en cuanto al tema de la inmigración ilegal a los EEUU? Incluya información del video para apoyar su respuesta. (2–3 frases)

[What do you think about the viewpoint of Mr. Fuentes on the topic of illegal immigration to the U.S.? Include information from the video in order to support your response (2–3 sentences).]

Theme: **Dandelion School Transformation Project**
(蒲公英中学环境转换工程)

Yu-Lan Lin, Boston Public Schools
Standards Addressed:
Interpersonal Communication
Interpretive Communication
Presentational Communication
Relating Cultural Practices to Perspectives
Relating Cultural Products to Perspectives
Acquiring Information
Cultural Comparisons
School and Community

Interpretive Task

Eight of your classmates spent last summer at a Study/Aboard program in Beijing China. They visited a migrant worker children's school called Dandelion School 蒲公英中学 in Bejing, China. They were deeply moved by the children and the school conditions there, and decided to organize a "community service" of raising money to send to the school. They wanted to involve the entire school community. Their idea of involving the entire school was inspired by the spirit of the Dandelion Transformation Project. You are going to first view the "Dandelion Transformation Project" on YouTube at home; then you will read an article written by Lily Yeh about the project and answer questions.

Interpersonal

You are going to be meet with a partner to discuss a fundraising project. In your discussion, remember to: a) set the goal of the amount you are going to raise; b) set the deadline by which the money needs to be raised; c) divide up the responsibilities for specific tasks for this collaborative work; d) plan for a presentation to compete for the "best " method proposed. Once the "best" fundraising method is voted on by your classmates, your class will make it a school wide campaign and involve the entire school community for this meaningful activity.

Presentational

You and your partner are going to propose a fun and efficient fundraising method via PPT. Your presentation is going to compete with other students to become the best fundraising method. In order to be chosen, you need to incorporate the spirit of "transformation starts from within," and "whole school involvement." You need to consider time and energy efficiency; you also need to think of incentives and additional benefits in engaging your school community in this fundraising campaign. You have ten minutes for this presentation.

Interpretive Phase: 蒲公英中学环境转换工程
Materials Needed: Prewriting activity, YouTube extract: *The Barefoot Artist Movie: Dandelion School Transformation Project*, interpretive listening text: *https://www.youtube.com/watch?v=afbFqdC5A9Q*, interpretive reading text: *http://blog.sina.com.cn/s/blog_4de325420100k9rv.html*, comprehension questions, pen or pencil.

NB. To retrieve the interpretive reading text, paste the above link to a Google search, click it and the text will appear below the blue color painting. Paste this link to a Google search and a Chinese link will appear, click the Chinese link and you will find the text below the blue color painting.

Prewriting Activity for Interpretive IPA Tasks
pair work (15 min)
View the Dandelion Transformation Project on YouTube at home sometime before class. (a Flipped Classroom activity) Read the following questions and think about how you would answer them. Once you are done, share your answers with a partner.

1. Who are the migrant workers?

2. Where do migrant workers come from? Where do they go to work?

3. Why do they leave their hometown?

4. What types of work do they find in the big cities?

Special Needs Adaptation:
1. Provide the pictures along with the text from the website for the students.
2. Read the passage aloud once for the students as they follow along on their paper. Students can then read the passage on their own before answering the questions.

Chinese Intermediate-High Interpretive Tasks (蒲公英中学环境转换工程**)**
Students read the following text and respond to comprehension questions — *individual work - 25 min*

姓名: _____   日期: _____

I. **Key Word Recognition.** Find in the article the word字/phrase词 in Chinese that best expresses the meaning of each of the following English words:

1. community: _____   6. stage show: _____

2. lively: _____   7. transform: _____

3. happiness: _____   8. art: _____

4. cooperate: _____   9. participate: _____

5. build : _____   10. judge: _____

II. Main Idea(s). Using information from the article, provide the main idea(s) of the article in English.

_____

_____

_____

III. Supporting Details.
- Circle the letter of each detail that is mentioned in the article (not all are included!).
- Write the letter of the detail next to where it appears in the text.
- Write the information that is given in the article in the space provided next to the detail below.

A. The place where the author has single handedly transformed a poor community to a 'paradise' in the US.

_____

B. The people with whom the author had experience working before the Dandelion Project.

_____

C. The type or kind of community project the author pursued in Philadelphia.

_____

D. Where the author wanted to bring her art project in the U.S.

_____

E. The type or kind community project that is difficult to attract the entire school community.

_____

F. According to the author, the kind of transformation that is easy to measure.

_____

G. According to the author, the kind of transformation that is difficult to measure.

_____

H. What the author believes that the Dandelion students can pursue in the future.

_____

IV. Organizational Features. How is this text organized? Choose all that apply and explain briefly why you selected each organizational feature—what were the clues in the text?
A. Chronological
B. Problem and solution
C. Description
D. Storytelling
E. Biography/Autobiography

Justification from text: _____

V. Guessing Meaning from Context. Based on this passage write what the following three words(字)/phrases (词)probably mean in English.

1. 转换 (in second paragraph) - _____

2. 壁画 (in second paragraph) - _____

3. 思维 (in fourth paragraph) - _____

VI. Inferences. "Read between the lines" to answer the following questions, using information from the text. Your responses may be in English or in the target language.

1. If the author thinks " 对由于外部环境的转变而产生的影响加以衡量并不困难" then, what does she think is difficult?

_____

_____

2. Why did Dandelion School provide an opportunity for the author to realize her dream?

_____

_____

VII. Author's Perspective. Select the perspective or point of view you think the author adopted as s/he wrote this article and justify your answer with information from the text.
A. Historical
B. Factual
C. Comic

Justification from text: _____

VIII. Comparing Cultural Perspectives. Answer the following questions in English:
1. Do you think a project like "Dandelion Transformation" can be duplicated in your school? Take cultural contexts into consideration when you respond to this question.

2. Compare and contrast students in the U.S. and students in China in terms of pursuing one's dream through action.

IX. Personal Reaction to the Text. Using specific information from the text, describe your personal reaction to the article, using Chinese. Be sure to provide reasons that support your reaction.

IPA Assessment Project—Presentational

Materials Needed: computers with Internet access, writing assignment, rubric, pen or pencil.

Teacher Notes: Two class periods should be spent on research. Try to have these two classes where students can use computers to access the Internet to get info they need for the project. Students should also bring their rough drafts one day before they are due so they can have their papers peer edited and checked for mistakes.

Prewriting
Students are to think about the following questions before they begin this task.
1. How can we reach out to the entire school community?
2. What kind of multi-media approach shall we use?
3. What are some of the incentives to get the entire school community involved?

姓名: _____ 日期: _____

Presentational Task
STUDENT PROMPT: You and your partner are going to propose a fun and efficient fundraising method through a PPT. Your presentation is going to compete with other groups to become the best fundraising method. In order to be chosen as the BEST fundraising method, you need to incorporate the spirit of "transformation starts from within," and "whole school involvement." You need to consider time and energy efficiency; you also need to think of incentives and additional benefits in engaging your school community in this fundraising campaign. You have ten munities for this presentation. In your presentation, include:
1. A formal greeting explaining the purpose of the campaign.
2. The goals of your proposal.
3. The outlines of your proposal.
4. Your reasons behind your proposal.
5. Your method of getting the proposal completed.
6. How does everyone in the community get involved in this proposal?
7. Why you think your proposal is the BEST
8. Thank the audience and seek their support.

SPANISH, ADVANCED LEVEL
Theme: **Divorce**

Instructor: Dr. Eileen Glisan, Indiana University
of Pennsylvania
Standards Addressed:
Interpersonal Communication
Interpretive Communication
Presentational Communication
Relating Cultural Practices to Perspectives
Relating Cultural Products to Perspectives
Making Connections
Cultural Comparisons
School and Community

Task Overview

In your Hispanic Cultures class, you have been exploring key societal issues common to both Hispanic and
U.S. cultures, one of them being divorce. You have been
doing research to discover similarities and differences
between the two cultures relative to divorce and the
impact it has on children whose parents have divorced
so that you can write an informed article on this topic
for your university's student magazine published in
Spanish. First, you will read an article dealing with the
consequences of divorce that appeared in a magazine
for adolescents published in Spain; it is similar to an
advice column. Then you will discuss the issue of divorce with a native Spanish-speaking college student via
Skype. Finally you will gather your research and write
your magazine article.

Interpretive

To have a deeper comprehension of the issue of divorce and
its impact on Spanish children, you are going to read an authentic article from OKAPI, a youth magazine published in
Spain. The article is designed like an advice column in which
an adolescent is asking for advice regarding his parents'
divorce.

Read the article and complete the accompanying "Comprehension Guide."

Interpersonal

After reading about and researching the subject of divorce and its impact on Spanish culture, you will have the
opportunity to interact with a college native speaker via
Skype. You will have a conversation with the native speaker
comparing and contrasting the impact of divorce in the US
and in Spain. During your conversation, try to find as many
similarities and differences as possible.

Presentational

Based on what you have learned from your research, read-
ings/discussions in class, as well as your Skype conversation
with a Spanish-speaking college student regarding the impact of divorce on children, write an article for your university's student newspaper published in Spanish. Remember
that your audience is the group of Spanish-speaking students
at your university and the purpose of your article is to provide an informed viewpoint about the impact of divorce on
children, which will serve to foster further discussion and
sharing of viewpoints on this topic.

Entre nosotros chicos

No tengo noticias de mi padre

Juan, ¡qué puedo hacer!

❝ Mis padres se divorciaron siendo yo pequeño. Mi padre se volvió a casar y se marchó a Cuba hace dos años. Un mes después regresó. Entonces me dijo que podría verlo cuando quisiera. Pero siempre era yo quien lo llamaba. Ahora ya no lo llamo y desde hace un mes no tengo noticias suyas. ¿Qué puedo hacer para que me llame? **❞**
Carlos, 11 años

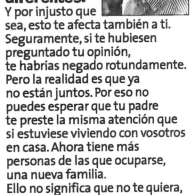

Desde que se divorciaron tus padres comenzaron a tener vidas diferentes.
Y por injusto que sea, esto te afecta también a ti. Seguramente, si te hubiesen preguntado tu opinión, te habrías negado rotundamente. Pero la realidad es que ya no están juntos. Por eso no puedes esperar que tu padre te preste la misma atención que si estuviese viviendo con vosotros en casa. Ahora tiene más personas de las que ocuparse, una nueva familia.

Ello no significa que no te quiera, pero debes comprender lo difícil que para él puede resultar tener otra familia y a la vez mantener la relación contigo. Tú lo sigues queriendo y por eso te gustaría que te demostrara también su cariño. A tu edad sigues necesitando de un padre y de una madre. Por ello tienes derecho a que tu padre se ocupe de ti aunque tenga que ser de otra manera. A pesar de todo él sigue siendo tu padre y tiene una serie de obligaciones contigo.

Intenta escribirle. Una carta puede ayudarte a expresar mejor tus sentimientos. Háblale sinceramente. No hace falta que le cuentes todas las actividades que haces cada día, pero sí hablarle de cómo te sientes, tus ilusiones, tus alegrías y penas... De esta manera él comprenderá mejor la necesidad que tienes de verlo y de que te exprese su cariño. Pregúntale por qué te olvida, si tiene dificultades para verte... Proponle la posibilidad de verlo, hablar un día y llegar a un acuerdo. Podríais, por ejemplo, quedar una tarde a la semana o cada quince días para ir juntos al cine. También puedes buscar la ayuda de otros adultos.

Pregúntale a tu madre; si ella guarda buenas relaciones con él podrá hablarle, a condición de no reprocharle nada, porque en tal caso puede perjudicarte. Si aún te relacionas con la familia de tu padre, podrías dirigirte a tus abuelos, a un tío o tía, hermanos de tu padre. Puede que ellos estén más cerca de él y le expliquen mejor lo que te ocurre. Como último recurso, si nada de esto funciona, habla con tu madre y dile que te acompañe para pedir al juez que intervino en la separación de tus padres que haga de mediador entre tu padre y tú. Le recordará su deber de educador hacia ti y le hará ver la importancia de mostrarte su afecto.

Eric Léal. "Entre nosotros chicos: No tengo noticias de mi padre," . Illustrations, Christelle Ruth, *OKAPI*, 9, May, 2002, p. 46.
Translated from"On se dit tout," *OKAPI*, 695, June, 2001. Reprinted by permission of Bayard Presse.

Spanish: Advanced Level Interpretive Task Comprehension Guide: Divorce

I. Key Word Recognition. Find in the article the Spanish word/phrase that best expresses the meaning of each of the following English words/phrases:

1. news: _____

2. left, went away: _____

3. as unfair as it is: _____

4. to look after, take care of: _____

5. maintain a relationship: _____

6. affection: _____

7. try to (do something): _____

8. feelings: _____

9. agreement: _____

10. last resort: _____

II. Main Idea. Using information from the article, provide the main idea of the article in English.

_____

_____

_____

III. Supporting Details.
- Circle the letter of each detail that is mentioned in the article (not all are included!).
- Write the letter of the detail next to where it appears in the text.
- Write in English the information that is given in the article in the space provided next to the detail below.

A. How an 11 year-old boy has been affected in school by his parent's divorce:

_____

B. Problem an 11 year-old boy is having with his father after his parent's divorce:

_____

C. The specific help that Carlos requests:

_____

D. Possible justification for the father's behavior, given by Juan:

_____

E. Information about Carlos's siblings:

_____

F. Why Carlos should write a letter to his father:

_____

G. How Carlos's mother might be able to help in this situation:

_____

H. Details regarding Carlos's relationship with his mother:

_____

IV. Organizational Features. How is this text organized? Choose all that apply and explain briefly why you selected each organizational feature—what were the clues in the text?

A. Chronological order
B. Letter/message
C. Compare/contrast
D. Biography/Autobiography
E. Problem and solution

Justification from text: _____

V. Guessing Meaning From Context. Based on this passage, write what the following three words/phrases probably mean in English:

1. te habrías negado **rotundamente** (2nd column, 1st paragraph): _____

2. en tal caso puede **perjudicarte** (3rd column, last paragraph): _____

3. podrías **dirigirte** a tus abuelos (3rd column, last paragraph): _____

VI. Inferences. "Read between the lines" to answer the following questions, using information from the article. Respond in Spanish.

1. ¿Qué tipo de niño es Carlos? ¿Cómo es su personalidad? Explique. *[What type of child is Carlos? What is his personality like?*

Explain.] _____

_____

_____

2. ¿De qué punto de vista intenta explicar Juan las acciones del padre de Carlos? Incluya información del artículo para explicar su respuesta. *[From what point of view does Juan try to explain to Carlos the actions of his father? Use details from the article to support your answer.]*

_____

_____

_____

VII. Author's perspective. Select the perspective or point of view you think the author adopted as he wrote this article and justify your answer with information from the text. Respond in Spanish.

A. Comic

B. Humanistic

C. Factual

Justification from text: _____

VIII. Comparing Cultural Perspectives. Answer the following questions in Spanish:

1. ¿Cómo se relaciona la información en este artículo con lo que sabe Ud. sobre el divorcio como un tema universal? *[How does the information contained in this article relate to what you know about about divorce as a universal theme?]*

_____

_____

_____

2. En su opinión, ¿qué semejanzas y/o diferencias habría entre la carta de Carlos y una carta escrita por un joven estadounidense? ? *[In your opinion, what similarities and/or differences would there be between the letter from Carlos and a letter written by a boy from the U.S.?]*

_____

_____

_____

IX. Personal Reaction to the Text. Using specific information from the text, describe your personal reaction to the article in **Spanish**. Be sure to provide reasons that support your reaction.

[Possible additional questions to elicit personal reaction:]

1. ¿Cómo respondería Ud. a los consejos de Juan si fuera Carlos? ¿Los seguiría? Explique. *[How would you respond to Juan's advice if you were Carlos? Would you follow it? Explain.]*

_____

_____

_____

2. ¿Qué le recomendaría Ud. que hiciera Carlos? *[What would you recommend that Carlos do?]*

_____

_____

_____

ARABIC, ADVANCED LEVEL
Theme: **Freedom**

Instructor: Myriam Abdel-Malek, University of Pittsburgh
Standards Addressed:
Interpersonal Communication
Interpretive Communication
Presentational Communication
Relating Cultural Practices to Perspectives
Relating Cultural Products to Perspectives
Making Connections
Acquiring Information
Cultural Comparisons
School and Community

Task Overview

Factors that affect the freedom of young men and women in the Arabic speaking countries

Before leaving to study abroad in an Arabic speaking country, you are studying about the factors that affect freedom of young men and women in Arabic speaking countries. To learn more about the factors you will read about the experience of a young Kenyan man and his Egyptian wife in Egypt. Then you will interview a native speaker to learn more about the factors. Finally, you will research the factors and present your findings to a group of students that are joining you in your study abroad program.

Interpretive

Before you leave to study abroad in one of the Arabic speaking countries and in order to understand some aspects of the Arab culture, you will read the article titled "شقيق أوباما في القاهره" From the reading you will infer some of the factors that affect the freedom of young men and women in Arabic-speaking countries.

Interpersonal

After your arrival to one of the Arabic speaking countries, you will meet and interact with native young men and women on a daily basis. You want to understand their opinions regarding the factors affecting their freedom. You will have a conversation with a native speaker about the factors that affect the freedom of young men and women in Arabic speaking countries.

Presentational

A group of students at your level of proficiency is arriving from the United States to study in the same Arabic-speaking country as part of your same program. To introduce them to the culture and have them understand the freedom of Arab young men and women better, you will give them a presentation. Based on what you read in the interpretive task, the conversation you had with the native speaker and your own research you will present the factors that you strongly believe affect the freedom of young men and women in the Arab world.

شقيق أوباما في القاهرة!

إبراهيم عيسى

إفترض معي أن المواطن الكيني المسلم حسين أوباما قبل أن يسافر في أوائل الستينات الى الولايات المتحدة الامريكية قرر أن يغير وجهته ويسافر أولا إلى مصر بلد الأزهر الشريف كغيره من مسلمي أفريقيا للتعلم والعمل في القاهرة عاصمة الاسلام.

جاء حسين أوباما ودخل جامعة الازهر تعرف على فتاة مصرية بيضاء من أسرة تعيش في حي حدائق القبة وأهلها أصلا من المنصورة , وأحب حسين أوباما البنت وأحبته وقررا الزواج. أهلها قطعا رفضوا الزيجة وقالوا:" مابقاش غير كيني أسود نناسبه!! ويا بنت مين القرد اللي حتدفني مستقبلك معاه؟" و إخوتها وأهلها قرروا مقاطعتها, أما أبوها فحاول بحكمة بأن يقنعها بأن الزواج من هذا الشاب الأفريقي مشكلة كبرى فهي ستلد أطفالا سود وسيألسن بنات خالاتها عليها, ثم إنه لن يجد عملا في مصر وربما سيعود الى كينيا (وتسيبي يا حبيبتي الحدائق وتروحي نيروبي. ثم الحب بيروح وبيجي – فكري في مسقبلك). لكن عناد البنت وحبها تغلبا على موانع وعقبات الأهل وتزوجت حسين أوباما الذي تخرج من الجامعة وبحث عن عمل في القاهرة خصوصا أنه أنجب إبنه مبروك حسين أوباما. لكنه بعد عامين كره نقسه من المصاعب التي صادفها وطلق الست زوجته المصرية وسافر مثلما كان يفكر في البداية إلى الولايات المتحدة الامريكية حيث تزوج فتاة أمريكية و عمل هناك وأنجب منها أبنه الثاني باراك حسين أوباما, ها نحن كلنا عرفنا ماذا حدث لإبن حسين أوباما الشاب باراك وكيف بارك الله فيه وصار مواطنا أمريكيا رائعا وإنتخبوه نائبا في الكونجرس الأمريكي ممثلا عن ولايته ثم تقدم خطوات هائلة نحو الحلم وصار مرشح الحزب الديمقراطي لمنصب الرئاسة حيث بات أول أسود يترشح لهذا المنصب في تاريخ الولايات المتحدة الامريكية وها هو على مبعدة أمتار من كرسي أهم رجل في العالم ورئيس مجلس إدارة الكون. لكن تفتكروا ماذا حدث لأخيه مبروك أوباما في مصر؟

أبداً حتى الآن لا يزال مبروك أوباما يحاول الحصول على الجنسية المصرية ولم يتمكن من الحصول عليها رغم أن أمه مصرية منصورية أبا عن جد. وهو دايخ في مصلحة الجوازات والجنسية للحصول على الاعتراف بمصريته أو تجديد الاقامة, كما ذهب مائة مرة لمقابلات في أمن الدولة حتى يزكون طلبه لوزير الداخلية بالحصول على الجنسية المصرية, لكنه لا يزال في عرف مصر أجنبيا كينيا حتى الآن وقد تعرض أكثر من مرة للترحيل من البلد عندما نشبت خلافات بين مصر وكينيا في وقت من الأوقات. كما أنه لم يتمكن من العمل في أي وظيفة حكومية لأنه غير مصري كما لم يستطع العمل محاميا رغم شهادته في القانون لأن النقابة لا تسمح للأجانب بممارسة المحامة أمام المحاكم المصرية وكان قد حفى بدلا من المرة مليونا كي يتم إعفاؤه من دفع المصاريف بالدولار في المدارس والجامعة طبقا للقرار الحكومي بالتعامل مع أبناء الأم المصرية بإعتبارهم أجانب!!

مبروك أوباما كذلك لا يصوت في الإنتخابات وليس له حق الترشيح طبعا لأي مقعد ولا حتى مقعد الحمام !

كيني أسود من حقه أن يصبح رئيسا لأمريكا أما في مصر فلا كيني ولا مصري ولا أسود ولا أبيض لهم حق الحلم بالترشيح للرئاسة. فالشرط الوحيد لأن تكون رئيسا مصريا أن تكون إبن الرئيس مبارك ... وهذا ليس الفرق بين مبارك وباراك أوباما بل هو الفرق بين الوراء و " الأماما".

Ibrahim Issa. "Obama's Brother." Used by permission of the author.

Arabic: Advanced Level Interpretive Task Comprehension Guide

شقيق أوباما في القاهره

Obama's brother in Cairo

I. Key Word Recognition. Find in the article the Arabic word/phrase that best expresses the meaning of each of the following English words/phrases

1. Destination _____

2. Obstacles _____

3. Convince her _____

4. Become relatives _____

5. Hated himself _____

6. Got elected _____

7. Representing his state _____

8. Renew the stay _____

9. National security office _____

10. Exempt from fees _____

II. Main idea(s): Using the information from the article, provide two main ideas of the article in English:

_____

_____

_____

III. Supporting Details.
- Circle only the letter of each detail that is mentioned in the article (not all are included).
- Write the letter of the detail next to where it appears in the text.
- Write the information that is given in the article in the space provided next to the detail below.

A. The reason why Hussein Obama's Egyptian family-in-law did not approve of their daughter's marriage to Hussein.

_____

B. Hussein left Egypt to settle in which country?

_____

C. Where Hussein Obama traveled before heading to the United States.

_____

D. The number of times Hussein Obama got married.

_____

E. Which one of Hussein Obama's children was born American and lived in the US as a US citizen?

_____

F. Who could be a president in Egypt?

_____

G. Who could never obtain Egyptian nationality?

_____

H. The position that Mabrouk was able to obtain in the Egyptian government

_____

IV. Organizing Features: How is this text organized? Choose all that apply and explain briefly why you selected each organizational feature—what were the clues in the text?

A. Chronological order
B. Pros and cons
C. Cause/effect
D. Compare/contrast
E. Story telling
F. Problem and solution

Justification from text:

_____

_____

_____

V. Guessing Meaning From context. Based on this article write what the following three words probably mean in English.

_____ تغلبا -1

_____ أنجب -2

_____ يترشح -3

VI. Inference: "Read between the lines" to answer the following questions, using information from the article. Your responses may be in English or in Arabic.

1. Why did Hussein Obama divorce his Egyptian wife? Explain.

_____

_____

_____

2. What is the message that the author wants to portray to the reader in the underlined sentence?

مبروك أوباما كذلك لا يصوت في الإنتخابات وليس له حق الترشيح طبعا لأي مقعد ولا حتى مقعد الحمام!

_____

_____

_____

VII. Author's perspective:
Select the perspective or point of view you think the author adopted as he wrote this article and justify your answer with information from the text
A. Informational
B. Moral/Religious
C. Social/Political

Justification from text: _____

VIII. Comparing cultural perspective: answer in English and Use the Attached Graphic Organizers (answer in English)

1. What are the factors that affect the freedom of the people in the article? Mention *three factors* for each of the following characters: a.) Hussein Obama's Egyptian wife b.) Mabrouk Obama – Using the graphic organizer, explain briefly how each of these factors affects the freedom of the characters.

2. Cultural comparison: Do the factors mentioned in question 1 affect the freedom of young men and women in the US? Why or why not? Explain. *Choose any three factors to answer this question.*

IX. Personal Reaction to the Text. Using specific information from the text, describe your personal reaction to the article **in Arabic**. Be sure to provide reasons that support your reaction.

Question 6-1, Part 2

Mabrouk Obama		
⬇	⬇	⬇
Factor 1	Factor 2	Factor 3

Question 6-2

| The factors which have an effect on freedom in your own culture. |

Factor 1	Factor 2	Factor 3

References

American Council on the Teaching of Foreign Languages (ACTFL). (2012). *Alignment of the National Standards for Learning Languages with the Common Core State Standards.* Alexandria, VA: Author. Retrieved from http://www.actfl. org/sites/default/files/pdfs/Aligning_CCSS_Language_ Standards_v6.pdf

National Governors Association Center for Best Practices, Council of Chief State School Officers (CCSSO). *Common Core State Standards for English Language Arts and Literacy in History/Social Studies, Science, and Technical Subjects.* (2010). Washington, DC: Author.

Chapter 7

Washback Effect of the Integrated Performance Assessment: Impact of the IPA on Teacher Perceptions, Classroom Instruction and Learning

Current research on assessment argues for a closer connection between instruction/learning and assessment. In other words, assessment should have a positive impact on teaching and learning practices (Bachman, 2007; McNamara, 2001; Poehner & Lantolf, 2003; Wiggins & McTighe, 2005). As discussed earlier, in Integrated Performance Assessment, real-life tasks grounded in authentic documents, models of performance linked to rich descriptions of expectations, and co-constructive feedback regarding the learners' progress work in tandem to connect instruction, learning and assessment. Accordingly, research on the Integrated Performance Assessment has revealed a positive and constructive "washback effect" on instruction; i.e., it can inform and improve the curriculum, teaching and learning practices beyond the test (Adair-Hauck et al, 2006; Adair-Hauck & Troyan, 2013; Davin et al, 2011; Glisan, Uribe, & Adair-Hauck, 2007; Shrum & Glisan, 2010). The washback hypothesis also implies that "teachers and learners do things that they would not necessarily otherwise do because of the test" (Alderson & Wall, 1993, p.17). Likewise, Rob and Ecranbrack (1999) stress the potential influence of tests and therefore encourage the creation of tests that will have enlightening effects on language curricula. Wiggins and McTighe (2005) argue that a test's validity should encompass the degree to which the test has a positive influence on teaching and learning. To this end, a goal of the ACTFL research project (1997–2000) was to investigate the washback effect or consequential validity (Messick, 1994) of the IPA on teachers' perceptions of their instructional actions and practices.

Washback Effect or Impact of Integrated Performance Assessment

As part of the ACTFL IPA research project (Glisan et al, 2003; Adair-Hauck et al), teacher reflections from follow-up questionnaires revealed that implementation of the IPA influenced the teachers' perceptions regarding standards-based language learning in a variety of ways. Over half of the 39 IPA Fellows responded to a follow-up questionnaire concerning the use of Integrated Performance Assessment. Questionnaire responses revealed that 83% (19 of 23 teachers) of respondents indicated that implementation of the IPA had a positive impact on their teaching, and 91% (20 of 22 teachers) reported that the project had a positive effect on their design of future assessments. The following comments reflect the degree to which the IPA Project influenced instruction and future assessment plans:

- Reaffirmed effective teaching techniques.
- Made me aware of the different modes of communication.
- Use more standards-based rubrics, those that don't lend themselves to objective grading, so the students will know exactly what is expected…
- Use or used IPA format in my class.
- Pay more attention to all-inclusive projects rather than ones limited by grammar points.
- The idea of the videotape is excellent, for students had the opportunity to discover their strengths and weaknesses.
- Need to do more speaking exercises/tasks.
- Through the rubrics, learned how to clearly assess my students.
- Look out for authentic materials/internet sources to use in this way.
- Incorporate the videotape interpersonal assessment.
- Use more spontaneous and open-ended type situations for them to create and use their language skills.
- Include integrated skills assessments.
- Learned a lot about designing questions for an interpretive task.

- IPA gave me a structure to follow for 2 person interviews—a logical application of paired oral practice.

- Will focus more on authentic reading materials and reading strategies.

- IPA informed me to include communication and content areas into my best assessment.

As illustrated by these comments, IPA training helped to raise the teachers' awareness regarding how to modify, change, or refocus some of their instructional strategies to enhance the language curricula. For example, the teachers cited that the IPA served as a catalyst to make them more aware of the need to integrate the three modes of communication into their lessons on a regular basis, design standards-based interpretive tasks using authentic documents, integrate more interpersonal speaking tasks, use more open-ended speaking tasks, and use more standards-based rubrics to help the students improve their language performance.

Regarding the challenges of integrating IPAs into the curriculum, the teachers reported: the lack of age-appropriate authentic materials; difficulty of preparing learners for interpersonal communication or teaching the students how to communicate and "think on their feet" without pre-scripted, dialogues; and difficulty of not being able to convert rubrics into letter grades for their school districts. This latter challenge regarding grades illuminates the depth of change that the standards and standards-based assessment imply.

Although these preliminary data from the teachers' reflections are promising, one needs to recognize, however, that the teachers' reflections are self-reports and just one piece of evidence regarding washback effect or consequential validity of IPA assessment. Further research studies including classroom observational studies, journals, and follow-up interviews will need to be conducted in order to ascertain if IPA training does indeed prompt teachers to modify and improve their instructional strategies and plans.

What follows are examples of how the IPA has had a positive impact on world language education in the states of New Jersey and South Carolina, as well as the observations of a few teachers who have been implementing IPA assessment for a number of years and who have contributed their IPAs for this 2nd edition.

Washback Effect of the IPA in the State of New Jersey

Cheri Quinlan

Coordinator of World Languages, International Education, and Gifted and Talented, New Jersey Department of Education (NJDOE)

New Jersey's entree into using Integrated Performance Assessments (IPAs) to assess student performance began in 2003 when four districts working as a consortium were awarded a Foreign Language Assistance Program (FLAP) grant to create assessment tasks modeled after the IPA. Through funding from the FLAP grant, teachers from the four districts received extensive training in standards-based teaching and assessment. Other world languages educators in New Jersey were invited to attend trainings when space was available. In subsequent years, Foreign Language Educators of New Jersey (FLENJ), the state professional organization for world languages educators, also offered several sessions on developing IPAs. These sessions were open to all world languages educators in the state. As capacity was developed for teachers to create and implement IPAs, districts began to incorporate IPAs as a way to assess student performance at the end of thematic units and as a component of or as the mid-term and final-exam assessments.

As resources were developed to support the 2009 NJCCCS (New Jersey Core Curriculum Content Standards) for World Languages, experts in New Jersey were recruited to develop a 21st century model unit that included an IPA as a summative assessment of the unit. Many districts have used that unit as a model for revising their curriculum to meet the 2009 NJCCCS for World Languages.

Through a State Education Agency FLAP grant focusing on a longitudinal study of student proficiency growth in ten New Jersey pilot districts, additional training has been provided to teachers to support the development of assessments aligned to the 2009 NJCCCS for World Languages. During summer 2011, more than 50 world language educators from New Jersey attended a three-day session on designing three-mode (IPA) assessments. Teachers from the pilot districts as well as teachers from other districts worked collaboratively to create IPAs targeting various proficiency levels.

In February 2012, the NJDOE embarked on a model curriculum project. At the present time, the Model Curriculum for World Languages includes the knowledge and skills necessary to meet targeted Cumulative Progress Indicators (CPIs), the smallest grain of the NJCCCS for World Languages, through the Student Learning Objectives (SLOs). Assessments to measure the SLOs are being developed for elementary and secondary students for the Novice-Mid and Novice-High proficiency levels. IPAs will be created to assess the SLOs at the secondary level. Although IPAs will not be used at the elementary level, the assessments will measure students' abilities to function in the three-modes of communication.

A recent anecdotal survey of world languages educators in New Jersey has shown that some institutes of higher education have made a concerted effort to include IPAs as part of a methodology course and/or require teaching candidates to create a thematic unit with an IPA as an important component of the unit. Many districts and teachers in New Jersey have also taken advantage of the numerous professional development opportunities associated with IPAs and embraced the use of them for mid-terms and finals as well as at the end of a thematic unit; however, there is still more work to do.

The professional development that has been provided through districts, the NJDOE and FLENJ, has helped to build capacity for world language teachers to move toward a system of assessment that focuses on what students can do with language in an authentic, real-life way.

Wasback Effect of the IPA in South Carolina

Ruta Couet
Education Associate for World Languages
South Carolina Department of Education

Since 2000, states have been creating accountability systems. In South Carolina, the non-tested areas such as visual and performing arts, physical education, and world languages were eager to provide schools and districts with criteria for quality programs in the absence of student scores from state tests, and so they focused on providing guidance for

program evaluation. In 2001–02 South Carolina high schools were invited to participate in an informal assessment of their world language programs by sending in curriculum guides and sample lessons and assessments. After careful study of the documentation, the review committee concluded that these samples demonstrated a lack of

- belief that language study is for all students
- consistency in curriculum guide format and usability
- consensus in program goals and methodology
- performance-based teaching & assessment
- professional development targeted to language teachers

Some of the participating schools, eager to improve their programs, requested templates for curriculum guides, lesson plans, and assessments. After careful consideration, the state committee decided that using the Integrated Performance Assessment (IPA) was the ideal organizing principle for curriculum development. Each high school was asked to submit a series of instructional units based on the IPA template. The lesson plans and formative assessments would be based on the developed IPAs.

The second pilot opened everyone's eyes to the level of implementation of the national and state standards. Considerable professional development was launched in 2003-04 and continues today in the Palmetto state concentrating on the three modes of communication, performance-based instruction and assessment, use of authentic texts, the culture triangle (products, practices, and perspectives), and grading practices. While modern language teachers avidly studied the IPA manual, Latin teachers expressed frustration at not having a manual and samples.

In 2006 the state approved a plan to evaluate one-fourth of the high school world language programs each year beginning in 2007-08 using the IPA as the template for curriculum development. Financing the necessary professional development and the cost of school documentation review is budgeted annually by the state. The South Carolina Foreign Language Teachers' Association (SCFLTA) continues to offer support in the selection of workshops and sessions at annual conferences.

Most building administrators have reacted favorably to this initiative as they began to see the benefits of a consistent approach to world language learning. Many districts undertook the development and use of the same IPAs in all of their high schools. Principals, assistant principals, and coaches began to view lesson plans and assessments as natural by-products of the established IPAs. The use of the IPA as the organizing principle of curriculum development launched a statewide dialogue about performance-based teaching and learning, assessment rubrics, and grading practices that continues to this day. When given the charge of revising state world language standards, the state committee chose to further strengthen the principles of the IPA by adopting the NCSS-FL-ACTFL can-do statements based on the *2012 ACTFL Proficiency Guidelines* in the 2013 *South Carolina Standards for World Language Proficiency*.

Wasback Effect: Voices of Instructors

Dr. Mandy R. Menke
Assistant Professor of Modern Languages and Literatures
Grand Valley State University, Michigan

Developing high levels of proficiency in Spanish has long been a goal for the Spanish program at Grand Valley State University. "Functional proficiency in the four basic language skills (listening comprehension, reading comprehension, speaking and writing)" forms part of our mission statement. Yet how does this play out in our day-to-day instruction and assessment?

When I reflected on this on a personal level after an Integrated Performance Assessment workshop in 2011, I felt that I did attend to all four skill areas and three modes of communication when teaching lower-level language classes (100- and 200-level). At the 300-level, however, I often only assessed the presentational mode of communication and on occasion the interpretive. I was also coming to realize that students often over-estimate their abilities and are generally unaware of their progress in developing proficiency. The Integrated Performance Assessment was not new to me. I had learned about the IPA model in multiple methodology courses and taught my own pre-service teachers about it, but I had never implemented an IPA-based unit in my

own classroom. During the fall 2011 workshop, I began to recognize the enormous potential the IPA holds, particularly in the area of providing students with feedback about their proficiency.

In the summer of 2012, I designed three different IPAs, two IPAs for students at the Novice-level to be implemented in a first semester Spanish course, and an IPA for students at the Intermediate High level to be implemented in a third year conversation and composition course. I was most excited about implementing the IPA in the third year course as students at this stage desperately need feedback about their proficiency development, and also because I recognized my tendency to focus on developing oral interpersonal skills and presentational writing skills.

When I developed my course syllabus for the conversation and composition course, I allowed time to conduct a full IPA at the end of the course, but I also incorporated a series of assessments modeled after the individual components of the IPA at different points throughout the semester. It was my goal to have two of the three modes of communication assessed during each unit of the semester. In this way, students familiarized themselves with the format and began to develop an awareness of what proficiency is. I found that by planning for these individual components throughout the semester, I more regularly assessed (whether formative or summative) interpersonal and interpretive communication. I also incorporated a greater variety of authentic texts related to the theme for each unit.

As an instructor, I was pleased with the outcome as I liked the greater incorporation of authentic texts and I felt like I better understood each individual student's strengths and weaknesses. Additionally, I began to recognize that my university students needed instruction on how to synthesize details from texts to identify the main idea. What I had assumed was the "easiest" mode of communication, the interpretive, continued to present them with a challenge; consequently, my instruction needed to address this. What most excited me was how students responded to the assessments. Through their comments, it became evident that not only did they have a sense of what they were able to do but they also were able to identify areas to work on in order to increase their proficiency. For example,

> "...when I am talking, I use many details and I also have fluency, but sometimes I'm lacking grammatical accuracy and also a logical organization with connectors. If I work to improve these aspects, my oral competence will move toward the advanced level."

> "...I was very surprised. I spoke with shorter sentences than I thought and with fewer connectors. I need to work more on my description and speak about more topics. I spoke with short words and I need to talk with more vocabulary and verbs."

Comments such as these confirm the power of IPAs to develop student awareness about proficiency.

Incorporating IPAs into my third year course had a variety of effects. Among the most important to me were the inclusion of more authentic texts, attending to a broader range of skills, and also developing students' ability to reflect upon their own proficiency and linguistic development. I implemented an IPA as a means of providing students with feedback about their proficiency, and while this objective was accomplished, my course design and instruction were also influenced for the better.

Myriam Abdel-Malek
Arabic Instructor
Less-Commonly-Taught-Languages-Center
University of Pittsburgh

I was introduced to the Integrated Performance Assessment (IPA) in a foreign language testing and assessment course that was part of my Master of Arts in Education program at the University of Pittsburgh. Since I was simultaneously exploring the assessment of culture in another course, I decided to explore the possibility of assessing culture using the three modes of communication. The IPA seemed like a highly suitable tool, given its focus on the National Standards. During the semester following the assessment course, I was assigned to teach "Readings in Arabic," a third year course at the university level. The course objective was to ex-

pose students to different genres of Arabic writing. I decided to use the IPA to explore the assessment of students' cultural competence. This required redesigning the course syllabus while at the same time meeting the course objective and my students' needs. Even though the course was designed for third-year-level students, in reality students in the class were at different proficiency levels.

Before making any changes to the syllabus, I looked for a theme around which to develop a unit of study. Keeping in mind that it had to be interesting for my students and had to expose them to cultural aspects from Arab speaking countries, I chose the theme "Freedom of young men and women in the Arab world", which would take about 4 weeks of class time. Coincidentally, I taught the course at the same time as the Arab Spring, which made it culturally and linguistically relevant and intriguing for my students.

The IPA had a major impact on the way I approached designing the course. With the IPA in mind, thinking of what I wanted my students to achieve at the end of the unit of study was the first thing I addressed. This was aligned with the concept of backward design. Normally, I would have chosen different texts from different genres and planned my lessons and then decided on the objectives and the method of assessment. However, with the IPA in mind my objectives were clear:

1. have students read and understand authentic texts around the theme of the topic and infer cultural aspects

2. have students use interpersonal communication to express their understanding of the topic in a culturally appropriate manner

3. have students prepare presentations related to the topic that shows their cultural understanding.

The second step was designing the IPA. Knowing I have students at different proficiency levels, I decided to assess them using the IPA Intermediate or Intermediate-High rubrics according to their levels. Here, the IPA allowed me to differentiate the assessment thus meeting my students' needs. This would have been difficult otherwise. Moreover, the IPA rubrics allowed me to focus assessment specifically on students' cultural competence by adding two cultural categories on each of the rubrics. These components, in effect, assessed the extent to which students met the standards in the goal areas of Cultures and Comparisons in the context of this unit of study.

The third step was finding authentic reading texts that students will work on in preparation for the IPA. Using the IPA influenced the choice of texts. Instead of looking for texts on different themes, using the IPA made the choice more focused. Thus it helped expose my students to the different cultural perspectives on the same topic from a wide variety of authors and genres. Normally, I would have jumped from topic to topic and students would not have had the opportunity to expand their vocabulary and cultural understanding of one topic.

The fourth step was designing the in-class activities. With the IPA in mind and the choice of texts made, the activities fell naturally into place. Again, the IPA changed the way I looked at instructional activities. Knowing that students had to practice the three modes of communication and at the same time discover the authors' cultural perspectives, the choice of those activities was more focused.

Moreover, the IPA impacted my feedback to my students. Previously, my feedback was focused on the correction of grammar and vocabulary. During the daily preparation for the IPA and the formative assessment linked to the IPA tasks, my feedback to my students was aimed at helping them improve their communication skills. Also, the IPA assessment-feedback cycle helped my students to prepare for each task.

In conclusion, the IPA impacted my syllabus design, allowed me to differentiate my assessment, and helped me give more focused feedback to my students. Being a firm believer that language and culture have to be taught as one entity, the IPA allowed me to address the culture goal and offered a tool with which to assess both language and culture through the three modes of communication. Overall, the experience with the IPA revealed that culture as language can be taught and assessed in relation to the context of a unit of study.

Dr. Michele J. Schreiner
Supervisor of World Languages and Spanish Instrcutor
Egg Harbor Township School District, New Jersey

I believe the decision to implement IPAs into our district curriculum was the single most pivotal decision to positively impact our curriculum. Four years ago, we were in the process of revising our curriculum from a textbook-based curriculum that focused almost entirely on grammar instruction to thematic units in the *Understanding by Design* format. We began implementing IPAs with all the level one teachers in French, German, and Spanish first. The subsequent year we added in level two, and added one level each year until we had revised our entire curriculum.

The impact from my perspective has been monumental, and I believe that the teachers who have been with the district longer than eight years (long enough to have taught several years under the previous curriculum) would agree. No longer are teachers as well as students focused primarily on paper and pencil assessments as evidence of what their students know; the teachers now have a clear focus on language functions and what their students can actually do with the language. By incorporating all three modes of communication, students are graduating with real communicative competence in the language. Interpersonal communication is practiced regularly. The teachers utilize a variety of methods to capture the students' interpersonal proficiency, depending on the unit and the teacher's preference. Most often the teachers utilize digital voice recorders and Google Voice.

I believe the implementation of IPAs in our curriculum has also had a profound effect on our students. No longer do our students have a skewed perspective of their ability in the target language. Students who used to get A's in their language class a decade ago often had little ability to speak the language because we taught students more about the language than how to use the language. That is no longer the case. By implementing IPAs into our curriculum and focusing on proficiency, our students now have a more accurate picture of their strengths and weaknesses in the language. One of the most noticeable changes is that our students now expect to speak in the target language both in class and on their assessments. Speaking is an integral part of every unit instead of something that is done occasionally.

José Pan
Spanish High School Instructor
Edison Township School District
Edison, New Jersey

ACTFL's Integrated Performance Assessment (IPA) model has thoroughly transformed how World Language is taught in Edison. Prior to the implementation of the IPA model, instruction at Edison High School was based on the paradigm of teaching, testing, and hoping for the best. Accordingly, our department sought to improve on the preponderant simple, rote tasks that had no meaningful function or benefit when it came to real world communication. Our department's desire to make communication our fundamental goal drove us to create Integrated Performance Assessments and implement them in our curricula.

The transition to this new way of teaching World Language was lengthy. It started nine years ago, under the tenure of our prior supervisor, Martin Smith, with a series of brainstorming sessions that lasted over three years. In these sessions, Mr. Smith, my departmental colleagues, and I articulated our respective visions for what the program would entail. These sessions, along with extensive training in performance-based assessment, proficiency, the development and use of rubrics and multiple district in-services, set the groundwork for us to start by creating benchmarks for the various language levels in our schools. Once we established these benchmarks, our next goal was to determine realistic expectations for students at each proficiency level. Defining expectations was the beginning of the transition towards eventually developing and incorporating IPAs into our elementary, middle, and high school curricula. A summative IPA is now the foundation of every thematic unit at every level of the World Language program in Edison. These IPAs enable our students to climb the proficiency scale by communicating authentically, as opposed to engaging in random and rote memorization of structures, grammatical points, and vocabulary.

One advantage of the IPA model is how well the thematic units created around each IPA lend themselves to the integration of culture, especially when teachers select solid, culturally valid, interpretive selections as the centerpieces of each IPA. These units immerse students in the target cultures, helping learners better appreciate the products, practices, and perspectives of people from outside the United States. The element of culture lends real world meaning to the study of language.

Integrating the IPA into our curricula has been a challenging but rewarding process involving many hours of articulation, curriculum writing, benchmarking, IPA creation, and implementation. As a result of our adoption of the IPA model, students in Edison now engage in language learning at a much deeper level than they previously had, and, consequently, form more significant connections. Ultimately, they communicate more proficiently and enjoy mastering a second language.

Tara Au Coin
French High School Instructor
Mahwah High School
Mahwah, New Jersey

Across all levels of my instruction, I have found that the format of the IPA interpretive task allows students to access the information and knowledge found in authentic texts more readily than any other line of questioning I have used. This has impacted my daily instruction in that I have adapted many of my interpretive activities to reflect this same line of questioning. In addition, I have found myself using L1 more often than I used to when generating such activities, as this really does resolve the problem of students copying or lifting information from the text that they do not genuinely comprehend. As helpful as this format has been for structuring interpretive reading activities, I must admit I have found it difficult to implement successfully when it comes to interpretive listening activities. In terms of the interpersonal mode, since my IPA training I have also made an effort to create interpersonal tasks that are rooted in the knowledge found in or questions raised by our interpretive activities. For me, this is another way to establish real world connections within the classroom and making in-class activities more meaningful for students.

Although I have held true to the structure of the IPA at the intermediate level, I have found it necessary to modify my approach when implementing this type of assessment at the novice level. Whereas at the intermediate level, students can complete an IPA in a span of a few days, it has been more effective, in my experience, to administer each section of the IPA separately at the lower level as we approach different phases of instruction. For example, I will have students complete the interpretive task to help them expand their vocabulary toward the onset of a unit, and then after all the targeted structures are addressed I will administer the interpersonal task. The presentational task would then be completed toward the end of the unit to display what students are able to do with everything we have learned on this topic. Based on the unit, the order in which I introduce the tasks varies, but I find that administering the IPA in this fashion is a way to hold students accountable without the pressure of three straight days of assessment, graded or otherwise.

Ashley Hellman
Falk Laboratory School, University of Pittsburgh
K-5 Spanish Instructor

After learning about the IPA and beginning to incorporate it in my own practice, I noticed that I also began to make some other major changes to my teaching. The most obvious changes were the way in which I developed curriculum and the manner in which I assessed student performance.

The first major impact that the IPA had on my teaching was that I began to incorporate backward design in my planning. In the past, I designed units by focusing only on the vocabulary, grammar, and activities that I thought fit within the unit of study. Although these items often related to the "theme" of the unit, I did not align these areas of the unit with the final assessment; therefore, many of the activities and much of the information did not truly support the content or skills the students needed for the final assessments. However, after learning about the IPA, I began to create units in a new way. Now, I begin by developing the IPA first. Then, I decide which content and skill sets the students will need to successfully complete the IPA. I incorporate activities that strengthen the students' knowledge and skills into my unit and make sure that the students are given enough practice working in each mode of communication. This ensures that the students have enough experience to successfully complete the IPA at the end of the unit. By using backward de-

sign with an IPA in mind, I now have a clear sense of the way in which I need to develop my curriculum. This definitely helps to simplify the planning process for me, and more importantly, it helps to make my students better prepared and more successful when completing final assessments.

The second major impact that the IPA had on my practice was the way in which I assess student performance. In the past, I often struggled to determine what I should assess and how to do so. After learning about the IPA, this became much easier for me to determine. I now focus on strengthening and assessing the students' interpretive, interpersonal, and presentational skills and I evaluate the students' performance by using rubrics from the IPA manual that are aligned with each of the three modes of communication. I also familiarize my students with these rubrics, and when the time arrives for the students to complete the IPA and other performance-based tasks within the unit, the students know exactly what is expected of them. I even adapted the students' report cards to reflect the three modes of communication, so the report cards are more aligned with the assessment tools used in class.

The IPA has definitely had a huge impact on my practice. It has helped me to more easily and effectively design a curriculum that is standards-based and developed with an "end" goal in mind. It has also helped me to better assess the students' skills and to provide the students and their parents with a clearer understanding of how the students are performing in my class. I know that the IPA has greatly benefited me as a teacher, but more importantly, it has also benefited my students.

Tracy Seiler, Ph.D.
President, South Carolina Classical Association
Latin Instructor, World Languages Team Leader
South Carolina Virtual School Program

When the South Carolina State Department of Education implemented a state-wide assessment of world language programs at the high-school level in 2007, the expectation was that all world language programs, including Latin, would be expected to utilize the Integrated Performance Assessment model. Latin teachers across the state were terrified, and as President of the state classical association, I felt it was incumbent upon me to explore this concept. In addition, the high school at which I was then teaching was one of the first to be assessed, and as I looked over the IPA manual, I realized that Latin was not represented there and that we would need to develop a slightly different set of expectations for the three modes of communication.

Traditionally, Latin teachers were never trained to speak Latin, unless it was to recite a poem aloud in meter, so the interpersonal mode was a daunting task to most teachers in our state. Additionally, our aims are different from those of the modern language teachers: our primary goal is reading proficiency. However, recent developments in Latin pedagogy have challenged the idea that one does not converse in Latin: cutting-edge college programs like that of Terence Tunberg at the University of Kentucky require conversational Latin, and summer immersion programs now abound.

With that in mind, we have revised our assumptions over the years. We now know that the practice of speaking and writing in Latin improves one's reading ability in the language, and to that end, I have designed my own courses here at the *South Carolina Virtual School Program* to include interpersonal communication using Twitter and Voicethread in every lesson. Students are encouraged not to translate Latin into English, but to read texts for comprehension and discuss their ideas, sometimes in the target language. While most of my students' communication with me and their peers is asynchronous due to the online medium, I have had recent success using Skype for synchronous interpersonal communication in Latin, and much of it is voluntary on the part of the students. As a result of using the language in this way, my students have become much better readers of Latin. In the years since I was introduced to the IPA model, I have come to realize that Latin is not so different after all, and that much of the model can be used with very good results in the Latin classroom.

Conclusion and Suggestions for Further Research

Teachers' reflections regarding implementation of Integrated Performance Assessment, as well as statements by the world language coordinators for New Jersey and South Carolina highlight that IPA training can serve as a consciousness-rais-

ing technique to influence or encourage teachers to modify or refocus their instructional plans to better meet the needs of students. To be sure, Integrated Performance Assessment is a ripe area for research. Research questions to be addressed include: *What is the impact of IPA assessment on language learner perceptions, motivation, and anxiety? After IPA training, do teachers follow through and implement their proposed plans to enhance the curricula? If so, do the enhanced curricula improve learner performance in achieving the standards? Does IPA assessment with co-constructed feedback guide the learners to become more reflective of their own language development? In what ways can IPA teacher training and implementation enhance school districts' efforts to link world languages with the Common Core States Standards initiative and the Partnership for 21st Century Skills?* Research that investigates these questions will reveal the potential of the IPA to change the way assessment is designed and implemented in language classrooms.

References:

Adair-Hauck, B., Glisan, E. W., Koda, K., Swender, E. B., & Sandrock, P. (2006). The integrated performance assessment (IPA): Connecting assessment to instruction and learning. *Foreign Language Annals, 39*, 359-382.

Adair-Hauck, B., & Troyan, F.J. (2013). A descriptive and co-constructive approach to Integrated Performance Assessment feedback. *Foreign Language Annals, 46*.

Alderson, J.C. & Wall, D. (1993). *Does washback exist?* Applied Linguistics, 14, 115, 129.

Bachman, L. F. (2007). What is the construct? The dialectic of abilities and contexts in defining constructs in language assessment. In J. Fox, M. Wesche, & D. Bayliss (Eds.), *What are we measuring? Language testing reconsidered.* Ottawa: University of Ottawa Press.

Glisan, E. W., Uribe, D., & Adair-Hauck, B. (2007). Research on Integrated Performance Assessment at the post-secondary level: Student performance across the modes of communication. *The Canadian Modern Language Review, 64*, 39-68.

Messick, S. (1994). The interplay of evidence and consequences in the validation of performance assessments.
Educational Researcher, 23(2),13-23.

Poehner, M. E., & Lantolf, J. P. (2003). *Dynamic assessment
of L2 development: Bringing the past into the future.* CALPER
Working Papers Series, No. 1. The Pennsylvania State University, Center for Advanced Language Proficiency, Education
and Research. 3-23.

Rob, T. & Ercranbrack, J. (1999). A study of the effect of
direct tests preparation on the TOEIC scores of Japanese
university students. *Teaching English as a Second or Foreign
Language,* 3, 4, 2-16.

Shrum, J. L., & Glisan, E. W. (2010). *Teacher's handbook:
Contextualized language instruction. 4th ed.* Boston, MA:
Heinle Cengage Learning.

Wiggins, G., & McTighe, J. (2005). *Understanding by design.*
Alexandria, VA: Association for Supervision and Curriculum Development.

Glossary

Assessing Question: A question that inquires to discover the student's ability to perform without assistance.

Assisting Question: A question that inquires in order to produce a cognitive operation that the learner cannot or will not produce alone.

Authentic Assessment: Assessment that mirrors the tasks and challenges faced by individuals in the real world.

Authentic Materials/Texts: Oral or printed materials/texts that have been produced by and for native speakers of the target culture for non-instructional purposes; e.g., newspapers, magazines, books, television programs, radio broadcasts.

Backward Design: An approach to the planning of instruction and learning that views the teacher as "designer" of assessment and instruction. In the approach, the designer (1) identifies desired results, (2) determines acceptable evidence, and (3) plans learning activities with the desired results and acceptable evidence in mind (Wiggins & McTighe, 2005).

Co-Constructive Approach to IPA Feedback: An approach to feedback recommended in the IPA Framework that involves the teacher and student in a conversation about the student's performance. The teacher and student view the student's performance, rate the performance with the IPA rubrics, and engage in a discussion in which the two identify aspects of the student's performance. Current performance is related to past performances. Likewise, goals are set for future learning. This approach to feedback is considered dialogic as opposed to monologic. In other words, the teacher and student are engaged in a dialogue regarding the student's performance (Adair-Hauck, 2003, Adair-Hauck & Troyan, 2013).

Cognitive Probes: Hints provided by the teacher which assist the learner to complete a task.

Comprehensibility: The degree to which a spoken or written message is understood in terms of whether only the teacher can understand it or whether a native speaker unaccustomed to interacting with language learners can also understand it.

Concept Inferences: The interpretive process of figuring out the author's intent by "reading/listening between the lines."

Discourse: Use of either oral or written language in communication that goes beyond the sentence level to paragraphs and conversations.

Domain: A feature or characteristic of a performance as defined in scoring rubrics.

Feedback: Information provided to learners about their strengths and areas that need improvement following or during a classroom activity or following an assessment. Feedback focuses on both meaning and linguistic accuracy

Feedback Loop: A strategy by which the teacher provides students with feedback on their performance after each of the three tasks in the IPA is completed, and before the next task is begun; this is an important feature of the IPA which uses a cyclical approach to second language instruction and includes Modeling, Practicing, Performing, and Feedback phases.

Framework for 21st Century Learning: A set of skills that has been identified as essential for learning to prepare students for work in the 21st Century. These skills have been linked to foreign language instruction and learning through P21 World Languages Skills Map.

Information Gap: A type of paired activity in which one speaker has information that the other does not have and vice versa, creating a real need for them to provide and obtain information through negotiation of meaning.

Impact: The degree to which a written or oral message maintains the attention of the reader or listener.

Input: A visual, oral, or printed message in the target language that calls for interpretation or reaction.

Integrated Performance Assessment (IPA): A theme-based assessment that features a series of tasks in all three modes of communication that support and build on one another. For example, a student might read an authentic text on the importance of maintaining good health (interpretive communication), interview classmates on their views about good health (interpersonal communication), and create an oral public service announcement with tips on ways to stay healthy (presentational communication).

Integrative Assessment: Assessment that combines the three modes of communication in a way that normally occurs in real-world communication.

Language Control: A characteristic of speech or writing that refers to the degree of accuracy, form, and fluency.

Language Functions: Language tasks that the student is able to handle in a consistent, comfortable, sustained, and spontaneous manner.

Interpretive Comprehension: The ability to go beyond the literal meaning of an oral or printed text to identify word inferences, concept inferences, author/cultural perspectives, and the organizing principle(s) of the text.

Literal Comprehension: The ability to identify key words, main ideas, and supporting details from an oral or printed text.

Modes of Communication: The three ways in which communication is characterized, emphasizing the context and purpose of communication:

Interpersonal: Individuals exchange information and negotiate meaning orally, whether face-to-face or by telephone, or in writing through personal notes, letters, and E-mail.

Interpretive: A reader or listener is engaged in understanding the meaning of oral, written, or other cultural texts (i.e., film, radio, television, newspapers, magazines, or literature) when the author of these texts is not present and meaning cannot be negotiated.

Presentational: Individuals engage in one-way oral or written communication (i.e., reports, speeches, or articles) that presents information to an audience for interpretation with no possibility of negotiating meaning.

Negotiation of Meaning: A form of interaction in which individuals work to understand each other and be understood through verbal requests for clarification, comprehension checking, and confirmation checking, such as "Could you repeat that?" "What do you mean by...?", "So you're saying...?"

Organizing Principle(s): The manner in which an oral or printed text is organized (e.g., chronological order, pros and cons, cause/effect, compare/contrast, story telling, problem and solution).

Proficiency: An assessment of performance of real-life functions, including the degree of accuracy and relevance of linguistic (grammar, vocabulary, syntax) and extralinguistic (including sociolinguistic) elements in a given context.

Proficiency-oriented Instruction: Instruction that focuses on the development of effective communication in all three communicative modes.

Responsive Assistance: The help that the teacher provides to learners to enable them to perform tasks that they may not yet have the knowledge or ability to do on their own. Also called Guided Assistance.

Rubrics: Written and shared criteria for judging performance that indicate the qualities by which levels of performance can be differentiated, and that anchor judgments about the degree of success on a student assessment.

Scaffolding: The process by which the "expert" and "novice" interact in a problem-solving task: the expert takes control of those portions of the task that are beyond the learner's current level of competence, thus allowing the learner to focus on the elements within his/her range of ability.

Target Culture: The culture of the people who speak the language being learned, including their perspectives, practices, and products.

Target Language: The language being learned in the classroom.

Text Type: The type of text used in an interpretive task at each of the three performance levels (novice, intermediate, pre-advanced) that exemplifies a certain level of linguistic complexity and topic familiarity; also refers to the quantity and organization of language discourse used by a speaker or writer (from word to phrase to sentence to connected sentences to paragraph levels).

Washback Effect: The influence a test or assessment has on the learning environment. Aspects of the learning environment include but are not limited to approach to instruction, assessment, curricular materials, student perceptions of learning, and student performance on the test or assessment.

Word Inferences: The interpretive process of figuring out the meaning of the unfamiliar words by using the context.

Zone of Proximal Development (ZPD): A concept defined by Vygotsky as "the distance between the learner's actual developmental level as determined by independent problem-solving (unassisted performance) and the level of potential development as determined through problem-solving under adult guidance or more capable peers (assisted performance)."

Appendix A *Inverted Pyramid Showing Major Levels of the ACTFL Rating Scale*

Superior

Can support opinion, hypothesize, discuss topic concretely and abstractly, and handle unfamiliar topics and situations

Advanced

Can narrate and describe in all major time frames and handle routine situation with a complication

Intermediate

Can create with language, ask and answer simple questions on familiar topics, and handle a simple situation or transaction

Novice

Can communicate minimally with formulaic and rote utterance, lists and phrases

Source: Swender, E., & Vicars, R. (2012). *ACTFL oral proficiency interview tester training manual.* Alexandria, VA: American Council on the Teaching of Foreign Languages, p. 7.

Appendix B   *Assessment Criteria Used to Assess Proficiency in Speaking*

Proficiency Level	Functions or Global Tasks	Context/Content	Accuracy/ Comprehensibility	Text Type
Superior	Discuss familiar and unfamiliar topics concrete and abstractly, support opinions, hypothesize.	Most informal and formal settings/*Wide range of public-interest topics and some special fields of interests and expertise*	No pattern of error in basic structures. Errors virtually never interfere with communication or distract the interlocutor from the message.	Extended discourse
Advanced	Narrate and describe in all major time frames and deal effectively with an unanticipated complication in a routine situation or transaction.	Most informal and some formal settings/*Topics of personal and general current interest*	Can be understood without difficulty by speakers unaccustomed to dealing with non-native speakers.	Oral paragraphs/ Connected discourse
Intermediate	Create with language, ask and answer simple questions, and handle a simple situation or transaction.	Some informal settings and a limited number of transactional situations/ *Predictable, familiar topics related to daily activities amd personal environment*	Can be understood with some repetition, by speakers accustomed to dealing with non-native speakers	Discrete sentences and strings of sentences
Novice	Communicate minimally with formulaic and rote utterances and produce words, phrases, and lists.	Most common informal settings/*Most common aspects of daily life*	May be difficult to understand, even for speakers accustomed to dealing with non-native speakers	Individual words, phrases, and lists

Source: Swender, E., & Vicars, R. (2012). *ACTFL oral proficiency interview tester training manual.* Alexandria, VA: American Council on the Teaching of Foreign Languages, p. 14.

Appendix C *Framework for 21st Century Learning*

21st Century Student Outcomes and Support Systems

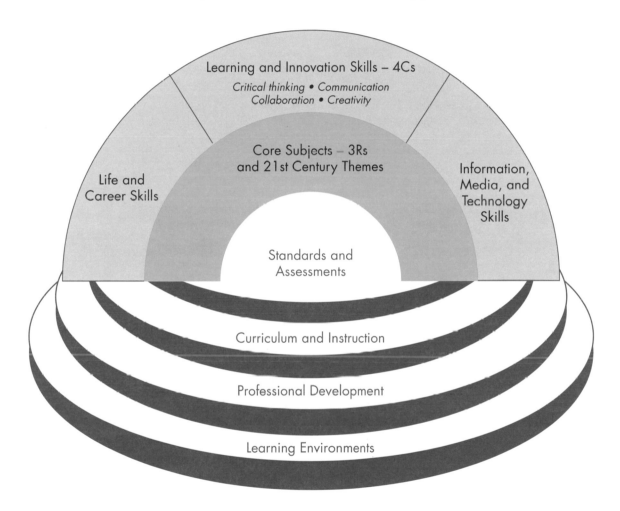

Source: Partnership for 21st Century Skills. (2011). *Framework for 21st Century Learning.* Washington, DC. Retrieved from http://www.p21.org/overview.

Appendix D   *IPA Interpretive Task Comprehension Guide: Template*

I. Key Word Recognition. Find in the article the word/phrase in the target language that best expresses the meaning of each of the following English words/phrases:

[Note to instructor: Select "content" words/phrases that convey meaning related to the text as opposed to words/phrases such as prepositions and conjunctions. Alternative format: Ask students to provide 8-10 words that relate to a specific topic or content area addressed in the text, such as nutrition.]

_____   _____

_____   _____

_____   _____

_____   _____

_____   _____

II. Main Idea(s). Using information from the article, provide the main idea(s) of the article in English.

_____

_____

_____

III. Supporting Details.
1. Circle the letter of each detail that is mentioned in the article (not all are included!).
2. Write the letter of the detail next to where it appears in the text.
3. Write the information that is given in the article in the space provided next to the detail below.
[Note to instructor: Provide 5 correct details that support the main idea(s) and 3 distracters.]

A. XXXXX - _____

B. XXXXX - _____

C. XXXXX - _____

D. XXXXX - _____

E. XXXXX - _____

F. XXXXX - _____

G. XXXXX - _____

H. XXXXX - _____

IV. Organizational Features. How is this text organized? Choose all that apply and explain briefly why you selected each organizational feature—what were the clues in the text?

[Note to instructor: Provide 2 correct answers and 3 distracters. Possible options may include: Chronological, pros and cons, cause/effect, compare/contrast, biography/autobiography, storytelling, description, problem and solution.]

A. XXXXX
B. XXXXX
C. XXXXX
D. XXXXX
E. XXXXX

Justification from text: _____

V. Guessing Meaning from Context. Based on this passage write what the following three words/expressions probably mean in English.

[Note to instructor: Provide three words that the student may not be likely to know but should be able to understand from the context. Provide the entire phrase in which the word/expression appears as well as a way to find it in the text such as the number/line of the paragraph in which it appeared.]

1. XXXXXXXX - _____
2. XXXXXXXX - _____
3. XXXXXXXX - _____

VI. Inferences. "Read/listen/view between the lines" to answer the following questions, using information from the text.

[Note to instructor: For Intermediate High and Advanced learners, create questions that require students to infer meaning by reading/listening/viewing between the lines. Write two open-ended questions such as: "Why do you think that...?"; "Why does the author say that...?"; "Why is it important that..?; What might be the effect of....?", which require inferencing on the part of the student. Questions may be in the target language. Specify which language students are to use and indicate that they must use information from the text in their responses. Note that some adaptations to this task may be necessary for lower-level learners, who may need more guidance in using inferencing skills. For Novice-level learners, you might give them a statement and ask them to list any evidence from the text that would help them to determine whether it is true or false, drawing on inferencing skills. For Intermediate-level learners, you could give them three inferences and ask them to select the best inference of the three by providing evidence from the text to support their selection, drawing on inferencing skills.]

1. _____

2. _____

VII. Author's Perspective. Select the perspective or point of view you think the author adopted as s/he wrote this article and justify your answer with information from the text.

[Note to instructor: Provide one correct answer and two distracters. Possible options may include clinical/scientific, moral/religious, humanistic, factual, historical, comic, etc. Specify which language students are to use in their justifications.]

A. XXX
B. XXX
C. XXX

Justification from text: _____

VIII. Comparing Cultural Perspectives. Answer the following questions:

[Note to instructor: Below are some possible types of questions, which may be written in the target language. Be sure to make reference to cultural products/practices, and perspectives in some of your questions. Specify which language students are to use.
- *What are the cultural similarities and differences between XXX and XXX?*
- *How do the practices/products in the article reflect the target culture perspectives?*
- *What did you learn about the target culture from this article?*
- *How would this article have been different if it were written for a US audience?]*

IX. Personal Reaction to the Text. Using specific information from the text, describe your personal reaction to the article, using the target language. Be sure to provide reasons that support your reaction.

[Note to instructor: This last section is designed to elicit a personal reaction from the student in the target language. This can be a bridge to the interpersonal task that will follow. However, this reaction is not assessed on the interpretive rubric.]

Appendix E

Why Do People Cross Borders?
Integrated Performance Assessment, Intermediate Level

French: Interpretive Task for La Société Québecoise Passage

I. Key Word Recognition. Find in the article the French word/phrase that best expresses the meaning of each of the following English words/phrases:

1. public : _____

2. to promote (v) _____

3. belonging _____

4. behavior _____

5. secularized (v) _____

6. live together (v) _____

7. citizens _____

8. elect _____

9. the right _____

10. opening _____

II. Main Idea. Using information from the article, provide the main idea(s) of the article in English.

_____

_____

_____

III. Important words and phrases. For each of the following,
- Circle the letter of each detail that is mentioned in the article.
- Write the letter of the detail next to where it appears in the text.
- Write the information that is given in the article in the space provided next to the detail below

A. The types of jobs presently available in Québec: _____

B. The number of languages spoken in Québec: _____

C. The accepted cultural practice for obtaining a service (e.g. the bank, movies, etc.):_____

D. With whom one usually uses the « tu » form : _____

E. How the Québecois culture prefers to handle conflicts: _____

F. The number of different cultural communities participating in Québec's society: _____

G. What the French language is a symbol of: _____

H. Why the people of Québec keep a certain physical distance from one another when talking: _____

_____

IV. Organizational Features. How is this text organized? Choose all that apply and explain briefly why you selected each organizational feature—what were the clues in the text?

A. Chronological order
B. Pros and cons
C. Description
D. Biography/Autobiography
E. Problem and solution

Justification from text: _____

V. Guessing Meaning From Context. Indicate the meaning of the following word from the context in the article.

Le système politique québecois repose sur la liberté (3rd paragraph): _____

Lorsque l'Etat entend légiférer (4th paragraph): _____

Ils gardent habituellement une certaine distance physique entre eux et leur interlocuteur… (2nd page, 3rd item): _____

_____

VI. Inferences. Answer the following question by providing as many reasons as you can. Your responses may be in English or in French. Use details from the document to support your answers.

1. If you were an immigrant or a refugee from the Democratic Republic of Congo, why would you want to immigrate to Québec ?

_____

_____

2. Compare the attitudes of Americans toward immigration and those of Québecois as presented in this article.

_____

_____

VII. Author's perspective. Select the perspective or point of view you think the author adopted as he wrote this article and justify your answer with information from the text.

A. Comic

B. Factual

C. Moral/Religious

Justification from text: _____

VIII. Comparing Cultural Perspectives. Answer the following questions in French:

1. Re-read two first paragraphs of the text. Relate this part of the text to the practices and perspectives of the French culture.

_____

_____

_____

2. What similarities and differences might there be between Québec's values and those of the U.S.?

_____

_____

_____

IX. Personal Reaction to the Text. Using specific information from the text, describe your personal reaction to the article in French. Be sure to provide reasons that support your reaction.

La Société Québecoise: Les valeurs communes de la société québécoise (p. 14)

http://www.immigration-quebec.gouv.qc.ca/ publications/fr/divers/apprendrelequebec.pdf

La société québécoise est régie par la Charte de la langue française que fait du français la langue officielle du Québec. Le français est la langue des institutions publiques et la langue normale habituelle du travail, de l'enseignement, des communications, du commerce et des affaires.

Le Québec tient à préserver et à promouvoir sa langue officielle. Le français représente non seulement un instrument de communication essentiel, mais aussi un symbole commun d'appartenance à la société québécoise.

Au Québec

- Le système politique québécois repose sur la liberté d'expression et le droit à l'égalité des personnes ainsi que sur leur participation à des associations, à des partis politiques, et à des instances administratives, comme des conseils d'administration. Les citoyens peuvent poser leur candidature à une élection et on droit d'y voter. Ils élisent leurs représentants à tous les ordres de gouvernement. (p. 15)

- Lorsque l'Etat entend légiférer, la population est généralement invitée à prendre part à des consultations afin d'exprimer son point de vue sur des questions d'intérêt public. (p. 15)

- L'expression de comportements haineux, qu'ils soient de nature politique, religieuse ou ethnique, n'est pas tolérée. La société québécoise favorise l résolution des conflits par la négociation. (p. 15)

- L'Etat québécois et ses institutions sont laïques. Leur décisions et leurs actions sont indépendantes des pouvoirs religieux. (p. 15)

- L'État québécois a déconfessionnalisé son système scolaire. L'enseignement religieux confessionnel ne fait pas partie du programme de l'école publique. (p. 15)

- Le Québec se diversifie. La majorité francophone, les anglophones et les autochtones cohabitent avec des gens d'origines et de cultures diverses venus de partout dans le monde. (p. 16)

Le saviez-vous? (p. 19)

1. La société québécoise d'aujourd'hui compte plus d'une centaine de communautés culturelles. De langues, de cultures et de religions diverses, ces communautés contribuent grandement à l'enrichissement social, économique et culturel du Québec. Elles vivent de manière pacifique et sont encouragées à entretenir des relations interculturelles harmonieuses.

2. Le Québec est une société où l'accommodement, le compromis et la recherche de consensus sont privilégiés. L'ouverture à la diversité, la tolérance et le respect sont aussi des valeurs très importantes entre les personnes.

3. Pour entrer en relation et communiquer entre eux, les Québécois préfèrent la simplicité. Ils communiquent généralement de façon plutôt directe, précise et de manière explicite. Ils gardent habituellement une certaine distance physique entre eux et leur interlocuteur, démontrant ainsi leur respect de l'espace personnel de l'autre. Le tutoiement avec les personnes plus jeunes ou d'âge similaire est largement répandu.

4. Les Québécois prennent généralement très au sérieux leurs engagements par rapport au temps. La ponctualité est de mise pour les rendez-vous.

5. Dans la vie publique, en attente d'un service, les Québécois respectent habituelle- ment le principe selon lequel le premier arrivé est le premier servi. Que ce soit dans un magasin, à la banque, à l'arrêt d'autobus, au cinéma, chacun attend son tour. La personne qui ne respecte pas cet usage s'expose à se faire rappeler à l'ordre par ses concitoyens.

Apprendre le Québec. http://www.immigration-quebec.gouv.qc.ca/publications/fr/divers/apprendrelequebec.pdf.
Reprinted by permission of the Minister of Immigration and Cultural Communities, Québec, Canada.

Appendix F *Integrated Performance Assessment (IPA) Rubrics*

Interpretive Mode Rubric: A Continuum of Performance*

CRITERIA	Exceeds Expectations	Meets Expectations		Does Not Meet Expectations
	Accomplished Comprehension	Strong Comprehension	Minimal Comprehension	Limited Comprehension
LITERAL COMPREHENSION				
Word Recognition	Identifies all key words appropriately within context of the text.	Identifies majority of key words appropriately within context of the text.	Identifies half of key words appropriately within the context of the text.	Identifies a few key words appropriately within the context of the text.
Main idea detection	Identifies the complete main idea(s) of the text.	Identifies the key parts of the main idea(s) of the text but misses some elements.	Identifies some part of the main idea(s) of the text.	May identify some ideas from the text but they do not represent the main idea(s).
Supporting detail detection	Identifies all supporting details in the text and accurately provides information from the text to explain these details.	Identifies the majority of supporting details in the text and provides information from the text to explain some of these details.	Identifies some supporting details in the text and may provide limited information from the text to explain these details. Or identifies the majority of supporting details but is unable to provide information from the text to explain these details.	Identifies a few supporting details in the text but may be unable to provide information from the text to explain these details.
INTERPRETIVE COMPREHENSION				
Organizational features	Identifies the organizational feature(s) of the text and provides an appropriate rationale.	Identifies the organizational feature(s) of the text; rationale misses some key points.	Identifies in part the organizational feature(s) of the text; rationale may miss some key points. Or identifies the organizational feature(s) but rationale is not provided.	Attempts to identify the organizational feature(s) of the text but is not successful.
Guessing meaning from context	Infers meaning of unfamiliar words and phrases in the text. Inferences are accurate.	Infers meaning of unfamiliar words and phrases in the text. Most of the inferences are plausible although some may not be accurate.	Infers meaning of unfamiliar words and phrases in the text. Most of the inferences are plausible although many are not accurate.	Inferences of meaning of unfamiliar words and phrases are largely inaccurate or lacking.
Inferences (Reading/listening/viewing between the lines)	Infers and interprets the text's meaning in a highly plausible manner.	Infers and interprets the text's meaning in a partially complete and/or partially plausible manner.	Makes a few plausible inferences regarding the text's meaning.	Inferences and interpretations of the text's meaning are largely incomplete and/or not plausible.
Author's perspective	Identifies the author's perspective and provides a detailed justification.	Identifies the author's perspective and provides a justification.	Identifies the author's perspective but justification is either inappropriate or incomplete.	Unable to identify the author's perspective.
Cultural perspectives	Identifies cultural perspectives/norms accurately. Provides a detailed connection of cultural products/practices to perspectives.	Identifies some cultural perspectives/norms accurately. Connects cultural products/practices to perspectives.	Identifies some cultural perspectives/norms accurately. Provides a minimal connection of cultural products/practices to perspectives.	Identification of cultural perspectives/norms is mostly superficial or lacking. And/or connection of cultural practices/products to perspectives is superficial or lacking.

Evidence of Strengths: Examples of Where You Could Improve:

* The Interpretive Rubric is designed to show the continuum of performance for both literal and interpretive comprehension for language learners regardless of language level. See *Implementing Integrated Performance Assessment*, Chapter 2, for suggestions on how to use this rubric to assign a score or grade.

Interpersonal Mode Rubric—Novice Learner

CRITERIA	Exceeds Expectations	Meets Expectations		Does Not Meet Expectations
		Strong	Minimal	
Language Function Language tasks the speaker is able to handle in a consistent, comfortable, sustained, and spontaneous manner	Creates with language by combining and recombining known elements; is able to express personal meaning in a basic way. Handles successfully a number of uncomplicated communicative tasks in straightforward social situations, primarily in concrete exchanges and topics necessary for survival in target-language cultures.	Uses mostly memorized language with some attempts to create. Handles a limited number of uncomplicated communicative tasks involving topics related to basic personal information and some activities, preferences, and immediate needs.	Uses memorized language only, familiar language.	Has no real functional ability.
Text Type Quantity and organization of language discourse (continuum: word - phrase - sentence - connected sentences - paragraph - extended discourse)	Uses simple sentences and some strings of sentences.	Uses some simple sentences and memorized phrases.	Uses words, phrases, chunks of language, and lists.	Uses isolated words.
Communication Strategies Quality of engagement and interactivity; how one participates in the conversation and advances it; strategies for negotiating meaning in the face of breakdown of communication	Responds to direct questions and requests for information. Asks a few appropriate questions, but is primarily reactive. May try to restate in the face of miscommunication.	Responds to basic direct questions and requests for information. Asks a few formulaic questions but is primarily reactive. May clarify by repeating and/or substituting different words.	Responds to a limited number of formulaic questions. May use repetition or resort to English.	Is unable to participate in a true conversational exchange.
Comprehensibility Who can understand this person's language? Can this person be understood only by sympathetic listeners used to interacting with non-natives? Can a native speaker unaccustomed to non-native speech understand this speaker?	Is generally understood by those accustomed to interacting with non-natives, although repetition or rephrasing may be required.	Is understood with occasional difficulty by those accustomed to interacting with non-natives, although repetition or rephrasing may be required.	Is understood, although often with difficulty, by those accustomed to interacting with non-natives.	Most of what is said may be unintelligible or understood only with repetition.
Language Control Grammatical accuracy, appropriate vocabulary, degree of fluency	Is most accurate when producing simple sentences in present time. Pronunciation, vocabulary, and syntax are strongly influenced by the native language. Accuracy decreases as language becomes more complex.	Is most accurate with memorized language, including phrases. Accuracy decreases when creating and trying to express personal meaning.	Accuracy is limited to memorized words. Accuracy may decrease when attempting to communicate beyond the word level.	Has little accuracy even with memorized words.

Evidence of Strengths: Examples of Where You Could Improve:

Interpersonal Mode Rubric—Intermediate Learner

CRITERIA	Exceeds Expectations	Meets Expectations		Does Not Meet Expectations
		Strong	Minimal	
Language Function Language tasks the speaker is able to handle in a consistent, comfortable, sustained, and spontaneous manner	Handles successfully uncomplicated tasks and social situations requiring exchange of basic information related to work, school, recreation, particular interests, and areas of competence. Narrates and describes in all major time frames, although not consistently.	Creates with language by combining and recombining known elements; ability to express own meaning expands in quantity and quality. Handles successfully a variety of uncomplicated communicative tasks in straightforward social situations, primarily in concrete exchanges and topics necessary for survival in target-language cultures. These exchanges include personal information related to self, interests, and personal preferences, as well as physical and social needs such as food, shopping, and travel.	Creates with language by combining and recombining known elements; is able to express personal meaning in a basic way. Handles successfully a number of uncomplicated communicative tasks in straightforward social situations, primarily in concrete exchanges and topics necessary for survival in target-language cultures.	Uses mostly memorized language with some attempts to create. Handles a limited number of uncomplicated communicative tasks involving topics related to basic personal information and some activities, preferences, and immediate needs.
Text Type Quantity and organization of language discourse (continuum: word - phrase - sentence - connected sentences - paragraph - extended discourse)	Uses mostly connected sentences and some paragraph-like discourse.	Uses strings of sentences, with some complex sentences (dependent clauses).	Uses simple sentences and some strings of sentences.	Uses some simple sentences and memorized phrases.
Communication Strategies Quality of engagement and interactivity, how one participates in the conversation and advances it; strategies for negotiating meaning in the face of breakdown of communication	Converses with ease and confidence when dealing with routine tasks and social situations. May clarify by paraphrasing.	Responds to direct questions and requests for information. Asks a variety of questions to obtain simple information but tends to function reactively. May clarify by restating.	Responds to direct questions and requests for information. Asks a few appropriate questions, but is primarily reactive. May try to restate in the face of miscommunication.	Responds to basic direct questions and requests for information. Asks a few formulaic questions but is primarily reactive. May clarify by repeating and/or substituting different words.
Comprehensibility Who can understand this person's language? Can this person be understood only by sympathetic listeners used to interacting with non-natives? Can a native speaker unaccustomed to non-native speech understand this speaker?	Is generally understood by those unaccustomed to interacting with non-natives, although interference from another language may be evident and gaps in communication may occur.	Is generally understood by those accustomed to interacting with non-natives.	Is generally understood by those accustomed to interacting with non-natives, although repetition or rephrasing may be required.	Is understood with occasional difficulty by those accustomed to interacting with non-natives, although repetition or rephrasing may be required.
Language Control Grammatical accuracy, appropriate vocabulary, degree of fluency	Demonstrates significant quantity and quality of Intermediate-level language. When attempting to perform Advanced-level tasks, there is breakdown in one or more of the following areas: the ability to narrate and describe, use of paragraph-length discourse, fluency, breadth of vocabulary.	Demonstrates significant quantity and quality of Intermediate-level language. Accuracy and/or fluency decreases when attempting to handle topics at the Advanced level or as language becomes more complex.	Is most accurate when producing simple sentences in present time. Pronunciation, vocabulary, and syntax are strongly influenced by the native language. Accuracy decreases as language becomes more complex.	Is most accurate with memorized language, including phrases. Accuracy decreases when creating and trying to express personal meaning.

Evidence of Strengths: Examples of Where You Could Improve:

Interpersonal Mode Rubric—Intermediate-High Learner

CRITERIA	Exceeds Expectations	Meets Expectations		Does Not Meet Expectations
		Strong	Minimal	
Language Function Language tasks the speaker is able to handle in a consistent, comfortable, sustained, and spontaneous manner	Consistently narrates and describes in all major time frames. Able to participate in most informal and some formal conversations on familiar topics, which may include current events, employment, and matters of public interest. Can handle appropriately an unexpected turn of events or complication.	Handles successfully uncomplicated tasks and social situations requiring exchange of basic information related to work, school, recreation, particular interests, and areas of competence. Narrates and describes in all major time frames, although not consistently.	Creates with language by combining and recombining known elements; ability to express own meaning expands in quantity and quality. Handles successfully a variety of uncomplicated communicative tasks in straightforward social situations, primarily in concrete exchanges and topics necessary for survival in target-language cultures. These exchanges include personal information related to self, interests, and personal preferences, as well as physical and social needs such as food, shopping, and travel.	Creates with language by combining and recombining known elements; is able to express personal meaning in a basic way. Handles successfully a number of uncomplicated communicative tasks in straightforward social situations, primarily in concrete exchanges and topics necessary for survival in target-language cultures.
Text Type Quantity and organization of language discourse (continuum: word - phrase - sentence - connected sentences - paragraph - extended discourse)	Uses connected sentences and paragraph-length discourse.	Uses mostly connected sentences and some paragraph-like discourse.	Uses strings of sentences, with some complex sentences (dependent clauses).	Uses simple sentences and some strings of sentences.
Communication Strategies Quality of engagement and interactivity; how one participates in the conversation and advances it; strategies for negotiating meaning in the face of breakdown of communication	Maintains conversation. May use communicative strategies such as rephrasing and circumlocution.	Converses with ease and confidence when dealing with routine tasks and social situations. May clarify by paraphrasing.	Responds to direct questions and requests for information. Asks a variety of questions to obtain simple information but tends to function reactively. May clarify by restating.	Responds to direct questions and requests for information. Asks a few appropriate questions, but is primarily reactive. May try to restate in the face of miscommunication.
Comprehensibility Who can understand this person's language? Can this person be understood only by sympathetic listeners used to interacting with non-natives? Can a native speaker unaccustomed to non-native speech understand this speaker?	Is understood by native speakers, even those unaccustomed to interacting with non-natives, although this may require some repetition or restatement.	Is generally understood by those unaccustomed to interacting with non-natives, although interference from another language may be evident and gaps in communication may occur.	Is generally understood by those accustomed to interacting with non-natives.	Is generally understood by those accustomed to interacting with non-natives, although repetition or rephrasing may be required.
Language Control Grammatical accuracy, appropriate vocabulary, degree of fluency	Demonstrates minimal fluency and some control of aspect in narrating in present, past and future time. Vocabulary may lack specificity. Speech decreases in quality and quantity when attempting to perform functions or handle topics associated with the Superior level.	Demonstrates significant quantity and quality of Intermediate-level language. When attempting to perform Advanced-level tasks, there is breakdown in one or more of the following areas: the ability to narrate and describe, use of paragraph-length discourse, fluency, breadth of vocabulary.	Demonstrates significant quantity and quality of Intermediate-level language. Accuracy and/or fluency decreases when attempting to handle topics at the Advanced level or as language becomes more complex.	Is most accurate when producing simple sentences in present time. Pronunciation, vocabulary, and syntax are strongly influenced by the native language. Accuracy decreases as language becomes more complex.

Evidence of Strengths: Examples of Where You Could Improve:

Interpersonal Mode Rubric—Advanced Learner

CRITERIA	Exceeds Expectations	Meets Expectations		Does Not Meet Expectations
		Strong	Minimal	
Language Function Language tasks the speaker is able to handle in a consistent, comfortable, sustained, and spontaneous manner	Narrates and describes fully and accurately in all major time frames. Can discuss some topics abstractly, especially those related to particular interests and expertise. May provide a structured argument to support opinions and may construct hypotheses.	Consistently and extensively narrates and describes in all major time frames by providing a full account. Participates actively in most informal and some formal conversations on a variety of concrete topics and topics relating to events of current, public, and personal interest. Can handle successfully and with ease an unexpected turn of events or complication.	Consistently narrates and describes in all major time frames. Able to participate in most informal and some formal conversations on familiar topics, which may include current events, employment, and matters of public interest. Can handle appropriately an unexpected turn of events or complication.	Handles successfully uncomplicated tasks and social situations requiring exchange of basic information related to work, school, recreation, particular interests, and areas of competence. Narrates and describes in all major time frames, although not consistently.
Text Type Quantity and organization of language discourse (continuum: word - phrase - sentence - connected sentences - paragraph - extended discourse)	Uses paragraph-length discourse and some extended discourse.	Uses connected, paragraph-length discourse.	Uses connected sentences and paragraph-length discourse.	Uses mostly connected sentences and some paragraph-like discourse.
Communication Strategies Quality of engagement and interactivity, how one participates in the conversation and advances it; strategies for negotiating meaning in the face of breakdown of communication	Converses with ease, confidence, and competence. Maintains, advances and/or redirects conversation. Demonstrates confident use of communicative strategies such as paraphrasing, circumlocution, and illustration.	Converses with ease and confidence. Maintains and advances conversation. Uses communicative strategies such as rephrasing and circumlocution.	Maintains conversation. May use communicative strategies such as rephrasing and circumlocution.	Converses with ease and confidence when dealing with routine tasks and social situations. May clarify by paraphrasing.
Comprehensibility Who can understand this person's language? Can this person be understood only by sympathetic listeners used to interacting with non-natives? Can a native speaker unaccustomed to non-native speech understand this speaker?	Is readily understood by native speakers unaccustomed to interacting with non-natives.	Is readily understood by native speakers unaccustomed to interacting with non-natives.	Is understood by native speakers, even those unaccustomed to interacting with non-natives, although this may require some repetition or restatement.	Is generally understood by those unaccustomed to interacting with non-natives, although interference from another language may be evident and gaps in communication may occur.
Language Control Grammatical accuracy, appropriate vocabulary, degree of fluency	Demonstrates full control of aspect in narrating in present, past and future time. Uses precise vocabulary and intonation, great fluency, and ease of speech. Accuracy may break down when attempting to perform the complex tasks associated with the Superior level over a variety of topics.	Demonstrates good control of aspect in narrating in present, past and future time. Has substantial fluency and extensive vocabulary. The quality and/or quantity of speech generally declines when attempting to perform functions or handle topics associated with the Superior level.	Demonstrates minimal fluency and some control of aspect in narrating in present, past and future time. Vocabulary may lack specificity. Speech decreases in quality and quantity when attempting to perform functions or handle topics associated with the Superior level.	Demonstrates significant quantity and quality of Intermediate-level language. When attempting to perform Advanced-level tasks, there is breakdown in one or more of the following areas: the ability to narrate and describe, use of paragraph-length discourse, fluency, breadth of vocabulary.

Evidence of Strengths: Examples of Where You Could Improve:

Presentational Mode Rubric—Novice Learner

CRITERIA	Exceeds Expectations	Meets Expectations		Does Not Meet Expectations
		Strong	Minimal	
Language Function Language tasks the speaker/writer is able to handle in a consistent, comfortable, sustained, and spontaneous manner	Creates with language by combining and recombining known elements; is able to express personal meaning in a basic way. Handles successfully a number of uncomplicated communicative tasks and topics necessary for survival in target-language cultures.	Uses mostly memorized language with some attempts to create. Handles a limited number of uncomplicated communicative tasks involving topics related to basic personal information and some activities, preferences, and immediate needs.	Uses memorized language only, familiar language.	Has no real functional ability.
Text Type Quantity and organization of language discourse (continuum: word - phrase - sentence - connected sentences - paragraph - extended discourse)	Uses simple sentences and some strings of sentences.	Uses some simple sentences and memorized phrases.	Uses words, phrases, chunks of language, and lists.	Uses isolated words.
Impact Clarity, organization, and depth of presentation; degree to which presentation maintains attention and interest of audience	Presented in a clear and organized manner. Presentation illustrates originality, rich details, and an unexpected feature that captures interest and attention of audience.	Presented in a clear and organized manner. Presentation illustrates originality and features rich details, visuals, and/or organization of the text to maintain audience's attention and/or interest.	Presented in a clear and organized manner. Some effort to maintain audience's attention through visuals, organization of the text, and/or details.	Presentation may be either unclear or unorganized. Minimal to no effort to maintain audience's attention.
Comprehensibility Who can understand this person's language? Can this person be understood only by sympathetic interlocutors used to the language of non-natives? Can a native speaker unaccustomed to the speaking/writing of non-natives understand this speaker/writer?	Is generally understood by those accustomed to the speaking/writing of non-natives, although additional effort may be required.	Is understood with occasional difficulty by those accustomed to the speaking/writing of non-natives, although additional effort may be required.	Is understood, although often with difficulty, by those accustomed to the speaking/writing of non-natives.	Most of spoken/written language may be unintelligible or understood only with additional effort.
Language Control Grammatical accuracy, appropriate vocabulary, degree of fluency	Is most accurate when producing simple sentences in present time. Pronunciation, vocabulary, and syntax are strongly influenced by the native language. Accuracy decreases as language becomes more complex.	Is most accurate with memorized language, including phrases. Accuracy decreases when creating and trying to express personal meaning.	Accuracy is limited to memorized words. Accuracy may decrease when attempting to communicate beyond the word level.	Has little accuracy even with memorized words.

Evidence of Strengths: Examples of Where You Could Improve:

Presentational Mode Rubric—Intermediate Learner

CRITERIA	Exceeds Expectations	Meets Expectations		Does Not Meet Expectations
		Strong	Minimal	
Language Function Language tasks the speaker/writer is able to handle in a consistent, comfortable, sustained, and spontaneous manner	Handles successfully uncomplicated tasks and social situations requiring exchange of basic information related to work, school, recreation, particular interests, and areas of competence. Narrates and describes in all major time frames, although not consistently.	Creates with language by combining and recombining known elements; ability to express own meaning expands in quantity and quality. Handles successfully a variety of uncomplicated communicative tasks and topics necessary for survival in target-language cultures. These exchanges include personal information related to self, interests, and personal preferences, as well as physical and social needs such as food, shopping, and travel.	Creates with language by combining and recombining known elements; is able to express personal meaning in a basic way. Handles successfully a number of uncomplicated communicative tasks and topics necessary for survival in target-language cultures.	Uses mostly memorized language with some attempts to create. Handles a limited number of uncomplicated communicative tasks involving topics related to basic personal information and some activities, preferences, and immediate needs.
Text Type Quantity and organization of language discourse (continuum: word - phrase - sentence - connected sentences - paragraph - extended discourse)	Uses mostly connected sentences and some paragraph-like discourse.	Uses strings of sentences, with some complex sentences (dependent clauses).	Uses simple sentences and some strings of sentences.	Uses some simple sentences and memorized phrases.
Impact Clarity, organization, and depth of presentation; degree to which presentation maintains attention and interest of audience	Presented in a clear and organized manner. Presentation illustrates originality, rich details, and an unexpected feature that captures interest and attention of audience.	Presented in a clear and organized manner. Presentation illustrates originality and features rich details, visuals, and/or organization of the text to maintain audience's attention and/or interest.	Presented in a clear and organized manner. Some effort to maintain audience's attention through visuals, organization of the text, and/or details.	Presentation may be either unclear or unorganized. Minimal to no effort to maintain audience's attention.
Comprehensibility Who can understand this person's language? Can this person be understood only by sympathetic interlocutors used to the language of non-natives? Can a native speaker unaccustomed to the speaking/writing of non-natives understand this speaker/writer?	Is generally understood by those unaccustomed to the speaking/writing of non-natives, although interference from another language may be evident and gaps in comprehension may occur.	Is generally understood by those accustomed to the speaking/writing of non-natives.	Is generally understood by those accustomed to interacting with non-natives, although additional effort may be required.	Is understood with occasional difficulty by those accustomed to the speaking/writing of non-natives, although additional effort may be required.
Language Control Grammatical accuracy, appropriate vocabulary, degree of fluency	Demonstrates significant quantity and quality of Intermediate-level language. When attempting to perform Advanced-level tasks, there is breakdown in one or more of the following areas: the ability to narrate and describe, use of paragraph-length discourse, fluency, breadth of vocabulary.	Demonstrates significant quantity and quality of Intermediate-level language. Accuracy and/or fluency decreases when attempting to handle topics at the Advanced level or as language becomes more complex.	Is most accurate when producing simple sentences in present time. Pronunciation, vocabulary, and syntax are strongly influenced by the native language. Accuracy decreases as language becomes more complex.	Is most accurate with memorized language, including phrases. Accuracy decreases when creating and trying to express personal meaning.

Evidence of Strengths: Examples of Where You Could Improve:

Presentational Mode Rubric—Intermediate-High Learner

CRITERIA	Exceeds Expectations	Meets Expectations		Does Not Meet Expectations
		Strong	Minimal	
Language Function Language tasks the speaker/writer is able to handle in a consistent, comfortable, sustained, and spontaneous manner	Consistently narrates and describes in all major time frames. Able to communicate on familiar topics, which may include current events, employment, and matters of public interest.	Handles successfully uncomplicated tasks and social situations requiring exchange of basic information related to work, school, recreation, particular interests, and areas of competence. Narrates and describes in all major time frames, although not consistently.	Creates with language by combining and recombining known elements; ability to express own meaning expands in quantity and quality. Handles successfully a variety of uncomplicated communicative tasks and topics necessary for survival in target-language cultures. These exchanges include personal information related to self, interests, and personal preferences, as well as physical and social needs such as food, shopping, and travel.	Creates with language by combining and recombining known elements; is able to express personal meaning in a basic way. Handles successfully a number of uncomplicated communicative tasks in straightforward social situations, primarily in concrete exchanges and topics necessary for survival in target-language cultures.
Text Type Quantity and organization of language discourse (continuum: word - phrase - sentence - connected sentences - paragraph - extended discourse)	Uses connected sentences and paragraph-length discourse.	Uses mostly connected sentences and some paragraph-like discourse.	Uses strings of sentences, with some complex sentences (dependent clauses).	Uses simple sentences and some strings of sentences.
Impact Clarity, organization, and depth of presentation; degree to which presentation maintains attention and interest of audience	Presented in a clear and organized manner. Presentation illustrates originality, rich details, and an unexpected feature that captures interest and attention of audience.	Presented in a clear and organized manner. Presentation illustrates originality and features rich details, visuals, and/or organization of the text to maintain audience's attention and/or interest.	Presented in a clear and organized manner. Some effort to maintain audience's attention through visuals, organization of the text, and/or details.	Presentation may be either unclear or unorganized. Minimal to no effort to maintain audience's attention.
Comprehensibility Who can understand this person's language? Can this person be understood only by sympathetic interlocutors used to the language of non-natives? Can a native speaker unaccustomed to the speaking/writing of non-natives understand this speaker/writer?	Is understood by native speakers, even those unaccustomed to the speaking/writing of non-natives, although this may require some additional effort.	Is generally understood by those unaccustomed to the speaking/writing of non-natives, although interference from another language may be evident and gaps in comprehension may occur.	Is generally understood by those accustomed to the speaking/writing of non-natives.	Is generally understood by those accustomed to the speaking/writing of non-natives, although additional effort may be required.
Language Control Grammatical accuracy, appropriate vocabulary, degree of fluency	Demonstrates minimal fluency and some control of aspect in narrating in present, past and future time. Vocabulary may lack specificity. Language decreases in quality and quantity when attempting to perform functions or handle topics associated with the Superior level.	Demonstrates significant quantity and quality of Intermediate-level language. When attempting to perform Advanced-level tasks, there is breakdown in one or more of the following areas: the ability to narrate and describe, use of paragraph-length discourse, fluency, breadth of vocabulary.	Demonstrates significant quantity and quality of Intermediate-level language. Accuracy and/or fluency decreases when attempting to handle topics at the Advanced level or as language becomes more complex.	Is most accurate when producing simple sentences in present time. Pronunciation, vocabulary, and syntax are strongly influenced by the native language. Accuracy decreases as language becomes more complex.

Evidence of Strengths: Examples of Where You Could Improve:

Presentational Mode Rubric—Advanced Learner

CRITERIA	Exceeds Expectations	Meets Expectations		Does Not Meet Expectations
		Strong	Minimal	
Language Function Language tasks the speaker/writer is able to handle in a consistent, comfortable, sustained, and spontaneous manner	Narrates and describes fully and accurately in all major time frames. Can communicate on some abstract topics, especially those related to particular interests and expertise. May provide a structured argument to support opinions and may construct hypotheses.	Consistently and extensively narrates and describes in all major time frames by providing a full account. Able to communicate on a variety of concrete topics and topics relating to events of current, public, and personal interest.	Consistently narrates and describes in all major time frames. Able to communicate on familiar topics, which may include current events, employment, and matters of public interest.	Handles successfully uncomplicated tasks and social situations requiring exchange of basic information related to work, school, recreation, particular interests, and areas of competence. Narrates and describes in all major time frames, although not consistently.
Text Type Quantity and organization of language discourse (continuum: word - phrase - sentence - connected sentences - paragraph - extended discourse)	Uses paragraph-length discourse and some extended discourse.	Uses connected, paragraph-length discourse.	Uses connected sentences and paragraph-length discourse.	Uses mostly connected sentences and some paragraph-like discourse.
Impact Clarity, organization, and depth of presentation; degree to which presentation maintains attention and interest of audience	Presented in a clear and organized manner. Presentation illustrates originality, rich details, and an unexpected feature that captures interest and attention of audience.	Presented in a clear and organized manner. Presentation illustrates originality and features rich details, visuals, and/or organization of the text to maintain audience's attention and/or interest.	Presented in a clear and organized manner. Some effort to maintain audience's attention through visuals, organization of the text, and/or details.	Presentation may be either unclear or unorganized. Minimal to no effort to maintain audience's attention.
Comprehensibility Who can understand this person's language? Can this person be understood only by sympathetic interlocutors used to the language of non-natives? Can a native speaker unaccustomed to the speaking/writing of non-natives understand this speaker/writer?	Is readily understood by native speakers unaccustomed to the speaking/writing of non-natives.	Is readily understood by native speakers unaccustomed to the speaking/writing of non-natives.	Is understood by native speakers, even those unaccustomed to the speaking/writing of non-natives, although this may require some additional effort.	Is generally understood by those unaccustomed to the speaking/writing of non-natives, although interference from another language may be evident and gaps in comprehension may occur.
Language Control Grammatical accuracy, appropriate vocabulary, degree of fluency	Demonstrates full control of aspect in narrating in present, past and future time. Uses precise vocabulary and intonation, great fluency, and ease of speech. Accuracy may break down when attempting to perform the complex tasks associated with the Superior level over a variety of topics.	Demonstrates good control of aspect in narrating in present, past and future time. Has substantial fluency and extensive vocabulary. The quality and/or quantity of language generally decreases when attempting to perform functions or handle topics associated with the Superior level.	Demonstrates minimal fluency and some control of aspect in narrating in present, past and future time. Vocabulary may lack specificity. Language decreases in quality and quantity when attempting to perform functions or handle topics associated with the Superior level.	Demonstrates significant quantity and quality of Intermediate-level language. When attempting to perform Advanced-level tasks, there is breakdown in one or more of the following areas: the ability to narrate and describe, use of paragraph-length discourse, fluency, breadth of vocabulary.

Evidence of Strengths: Examples of Where You Could Improve:

Appendix G *Sample Formative Assessment*

Directions: Throughout this unit "Why Do People Cross Borders," you will meet many different people from the community. To prepare for these interactions and for the interpersonal task on the IPA at the end of this unit, you will complete a role play activity at the beginning of class each day. You will take on a new identity each day. This is your identity today. Take notes about the information that you learn about the person you've met in town today because you will enter these notes into an on-going journal.

(Note the teacher: Cut the task sheet in half and give one identity to Student A and another to student B).

Daily Speaking Task

Student A From _____	Student B From Vietnam
	• Parents died in 1977 • Came to the U.S. for work in 1978. • Returned to Vietnam last year for the first time. • Found there his long-lost sweetheart who was then married. *Ask three questions of your partner.*

Daily Speaking Task

Student A From Rwanda	Student B From _____
• Came to the United States in 2003. • Was a refugee from Rwanda. • Worked as a doctor in Rwanda. • Had to begin a whole new career because her degree was not recognized here. *Ask three questions of your partner.*	

Appendix H   *Vocabulary Matrix to Promote the Negotiation of Meaning*

To promote the active negotiation of meaning in interpersonal speaking, students use the framework below to organize vocabulary from the beginning of study in the French program. The approach reflects facets of instruction that include providing comprehensible input using images and gestures and by expressing oneself "in other words". Eventually, as is the case in this example, students create personalized vocabulary lists using the matrix.

Nom _____

Mon Dictionnaire: Histoire d'immigration

Mot	Image	En autres mots...

Source: F. Troyan original document.

Appendix I

Feedback Loop: Key Feature of the Cyclical Approach
Explicit vs Co-Constructive Feedback for the Interpretive Mode
by Bonnie Adair-Hauck, Ph.D.

The feedback loop is an excellent opportunity to assist the students' understanding of the interpretive text before they go to the next phase of the IPA. Additionally, if the teacher provides responsive assistance during the feedback loop, the students can gain a better understanding of **how to improve their performance on the next IPA.**

After the teacher has corrected the students' responses for the interpretive tasks, s/he is equipped with a comprehensive understanding of which tasks the *students can perform on their own,* and which tasks are challenging and require *responsive assistance on the part of the teacher.* For example, after correcting the interpretive responses, the teacher notices that many of the students did well on two sections of intermediate level tasks: main idea and supporting details. However, the students did not perform nearly as well on the "guessing meaning from context" tasks. Enlightened with this critical information, the teacher has a rich opportunity to work within the students' *zone of proximal development during the feedback loop.* Recall that learners bring two levels of cognitive development when faced with problem-solving tasks: an actual level, that is, tasks which they can perform unassisted; and a potential developmental level, which denotes what students may be able to do with assistance. Vygotsky defined the ZPD as "the distance between the learner's actual developmental level as determined by independent problem-solving (unassisted performance) and the level of potential development as determined through problem-solving under adult guidance or more capable peers (assisted performance)." Vygotsky, 1978, p. 86.

In other words, enlightened by the IPA interpretive responses, the teacher now understands which tasks the students can *perform by themselves,* and *which tasks require assistance.* With this information, the teacher can set the stage for an enriching instructional interaction during the feedback loop. Using assisting questions, and cognitive probes (Tharp &

Gallimore, 1988), the teacher guides the students to become more aware of the various reading strategies that may be used to solve interpretive tasks. The feedback loop will be more beneficial and productive if the teacher provides cognitively challenging and co-constructive feedback rather than explicit feedback (Adair-Hauck and Donato, 1994). The following two protocols highlight the differences between explicit and responsive/co-constructive teacher feedback. The protocols refer to the French Intermediate IPA on "Your Health".

Explicit Teacher Feedback

(T) Most of you had difficulty with Section III, "Guessing Meaning from Context". We better go over these. Who knows the answer to Question 1, "en allumant"? It can be found in the first paragraph. Jeff?

(S1) "I didn't get that one".

(T)   OK. Susan?

(S2) I think it means "opening".

(T) No, it doesn't mean "opening". "En ouvrant" means "while opening" that's in the sentence above. Trevor, you did well on this section. What's your answer.

(S3) "I put down 'while lighting'.

(T) Correct. It comes from the verb – "allumer" which means "to light" or in this case, "turn on or light the lamps". OK. Let's go on to number 2. Annie?

(S4) I didn't get that one. Ok. Sam?

Responsive and Co-Constructive Feedback to Improve Student Performance

(T)   Most of the class had difficulty with Section III – "Guessing Meaning from Context." This is a difficult section, and that is why it is considered to be a task that falls into the "exceeds expectations" category. But if you want to become better readers, we need to have strategies for guessing meaning from context. Let's try to figure out how to solve these "guessing meaning from context" questions so that you'll do better the next time.

(T)   Look at question 1, "en allumant" which is in the first paragraph. How can we try to guess the meaning of that word? First, think to yourselves about some ways that you can make an educative guess about the meaning of this word. (give students some time to reflect on possible strategies).

(T)   OK. Any suggestions on how we can guess the meaning of this word? Julie?

(S1) I looked at the picture right next to that paragraph. It's morning time. The woman is opening the curtain, she's letting in the sunlight.

(T)   Yes. Good strategy. There's a picture to support your understanding and to help you understand the meaning of this paragraph.

(T)   Other suggestions for ways to find the answer? Ray?

(S2) I think it's a verb. It looks like a verb.

(T)   Good clue. Yes, it is a verb , and if it's a verb it's referring to what, Ray.

(S2) Oh, an action, a verb refers to some sort of action.

(T)   Yes, what makes you think that it's a verb or action word, Ray.

(S2) It's preceded by the little word "en" just like "en ouvrant" which is in the same sentence. I know "en ouvant" means "while opening", but I'm not sure of "en allumant".

(T)   We're on the right track. It's definitely a verb or an action word. There's still another reading strategy that can help us solve this question. What else can we do to try to guess the meaning of the new words, besides looking at the pictures and figuring out the part of speech? Jake?

(S3) I looked at the other words in the sentence: "en allumant les halogènes". I know that "halogènes" means "lights" or lamps in English—and it makes sense "to light", or "turn on the lamps", in the morning.

(T)   Exactly. You looked at the other words in the sentence and guessed what would make sense from those contextual clues. We're starting to understand that there are multiple ways for trying to guess the meanings of these words. I'm curious too. Do any of you see a connection between a word in the subtitle and "en allumant"? Larry?

(S4) "Lumineuse" and "allumant" ?

(T)   Yes, that's it. Now what's the connection?

(S4) They both have the stem "lum" .

(T)   Good – and can anyone think of an English word with "lum" that we use frequently around the holidays.

(SS) A few students respond in unison "luminaries!".

(T)   Great. You're catching on now. Now, let's try number 2. First, take a minute to reflect and see if you can find the meaning of the word: "tartiné". Share your predictions with a neighbor.

Commentary: The explicit feedback protocol exemplifies a didactic or "automatic" exchange with questions that mainly assess students' knowledge. With these types of questions, the students are given little opportunity to improve their performance from the feedback. On the other hand, the responsive and co-constructive feedback protocol represents joint problem-solving on the part of the teacher and learners. To do so, the teacher scaffolds the task by using both assisting as well as assessing questions (see definitions below). The teacher scaffolds the problem by holding the task difficulty constant, while simplifying the students' role by means of graduated assistance (Greenfield, 1984). This scaffolded assistance allows that learners to participate in activities that would be too difficult to perform without assistance from an expert or more capable peer.

As Vygotsky reminds us: "Teaching is effective only when it *awakens and rouses to life those functions which are in a stage of maturing, which lie in the zone of proximal development. Teaching must be aimed not so much at the ripe, but at the ripening functions.* (italics in original)" Vygotsky, 1986, p. 278.

(reprinted from ACTFL IPA Manual, *p. 12-15)*

*** "assessing question: inquires to discover the student's ability to perform without assistance (e.g., to establish what the students may remember from yesterday's lesson)." Tharp and Gallimore, 1988, p. 59.

*** "assisting question: inquires in order to produce a cognitive operation that the learner can not or will not produce alone. The assistance provided by the question prompts the mental operation" Tharp and Gallimore, 1988, p. 60.

Additional citations:

Adair-Hauck, B. and Donato, R. (1994). Foreign language explanations within the zone of proximal development. *Canadian Modern Language Review*, 50, 532-557.

Greenfield, P. (1984). A theory of the teacher in learning activities of everyday life. In B. Rogoff & J. Lave (Eds.), *Everyday cognition: Its development in social contexts* (pp.117-138). Cambrdge, MA: Harvard University Press.

Tharp, R. and Gallimore, R. (1988). *Rousing minds to life: Teaching, learning and schooling in social contexts.* Cambridge, MA: Cambridge University Press.

Vygotsky, L.S. (1978). Mind in society: The development of higher psychological processes. (M. Cole, V. John-Steiner, S. Scribner & E. Souberman, Eds. & Trans.) Cambridge, MA: Harvard University Press.

Vygotsky, L.S. (1986). Thought and Language. Cambridge:MA MIT Press.

Appendix J *Sample Co-Constructive Feedback for "Does Not Meet Expectations"*

Communication Standard 1.1 – Interpersonal Communication, Intermediate Level

T: So based on what we've just watched, where would you put yourself, um, starting at the top [of the rubric]?

> Assisting question to encourage student to self-assess

S: Well basically everything I said was memorized from the paper that I had written up about her for my biography.

T: Okay

S: For text type, again they're just kind of memorized phrases that I just saw. Like I kind of like just saw it quickly and just tried to remember what it was. Remembering like the wording of it.

> Student acknowledges text type limited to memorized phrases

T: Okay. And what could you do to prepare? To be able to talk more about her?

> Assisting question to encourage student to think of strategies to prepare for task

S: Well one thing I'm not really sure how to do is like… because I don't really know her…at all all. So, I…I haven't really seen any movies with her in them. So I don't even know who she is.

> Student notes his lack of knowledge

T: Uh huh.

S: And all I know is the information that I found out on the internet. So, I'm not really sure how I can like expand on who she is because I have no idea…like…I've never heard of her before.

> Again student notes his lack of content

T: Okay. So, what made you choose her?

> Assisting question on why student chose this famous person

S: What made? Well because I looked up…I just typed in "French celebrities" and a big list came up and I just picked her name from the list.

> Student states it was by chance

T: Okay. So, knowing that there are, for example, at (local video rental store) two films that you could rent what could you do to prep(pare)?

> Teacher providing "hints" about movies and assisting question on how student could prepare

S: Go watch them.

> Student is co-constructing strategies and plans

T: And as you're watching them, what will you be looking for?

> Assisting question to guide student "thinking" as he is watching the film

S: Personal qualities and traits and things like that I guess.

> Student co-constructing plan

T: Okay. And um…what as…so if you watch one or two of her movies, what could you then bring back this conversation?

> Assisting question on content of film

S: Um…the kind of actor she is. The kind of roles she plays.

> Student co-constructing plan

T: Okay. And what else? How could you…what about what is actually happening in the movie?

> Assisting question to help student think about plot of the film

S: Like what? What do you mean?

> Clarification question by student

T: Um…could you talk about the film as well? ——————— Teacher provides answer regarding plot of film

S: Yeah. Yeah. Most likely. ——————— Student agrees

T: How would you do that? ——————— Assisting question to encourage student

S: I would just be like, "At this part, she was like this" ——————— Student co-constructing plan
   or whatever.

T: Alright. So you could just narrate an interesting part ——————— Teacher assisting by expanding idea
   of the film.

S: Yeah

T: Ah…coming down here (points to the Communication ——————— Teacher focuses on Communication Strategies
   Strategies row of the rubric), did you, ah, did you ask
   any questions?

S: No, she basically like made sure that she was using really
   simple things so that I would understand her.

T: Okay. So, I…the other thing is I think you'll definitely have
   a different partner the next time that you do it.

S: Yeah so I'll have to ask more questions. ——————— Student acknowledging that he will have to ask more questions

T: Right. So you'd have to ask more questions and depending
   on…So it would be interesting to see how it goes with someone who…is a native speaker and able to fill in a lot of gaps
   for you.

S: As opposed to a person who doesn't know how to do
   that much.

T: So your plan to prep[are] is what? ——————— Assessing question to encourage student to recap plan to succeed

S: I'll go rent *The Da Vinci Code*. ——————— Student states how to start plan

T: Okay. And there's also the film *Amélie*. ——————— Teacher co-constructing plan

S: Mm hmm.

T: Okay? Um. And…that would be another good one
   to check out.

S: Okay.

T: Okay? And we'll give it another shot.

Permissions and Credits

The authors wish to thank the following persons and publishers for permission to use their articles or illustrations included in this publication.

Chapter 4

page 29–30: G. Wiggins and J. McTighe (2005). *Understanding by design* (expanded 2nd ed.). Alexandria, VA: Association for Supervision and Curriculum Development. Template adapted and reprinted with permission from the authors.

page 35: José Molina. "Laura Esquivel: Mucho más que un 'patito feo,'" *OKAPI*, 98, October, 2010, p. 50. Reprinted with permission (text only) of Bayard-Revistas.

Chapter 6

page 60: *El Recinto de Río Piedras de la Universidad de Puerto Rico*. http://www.upr.edu/?type=page&id=recintos_RioPiedras&ancla=RioPiedras. Reprinted with permission by University of Puerto Rico, Committee of Intellectual Property.

page 69–70: Mathieu Rocher. "L'écolo dico rigolo," *ASTRAPI*, 770, April 2012, p.2-7. Illustrations, Marion Puech. Graphics, Lorraine Harris. Reprinted by permission of Bayard Presse.

page 90: Eric Léal. "Entre nosotros chicos: No tengo noticias de mi padre." Illustrations, Christelle Ruth, *OKAPI*, 9, May, 2002, p. 46. Translated from "On se dit tout," *OKAPI*, 695, June, 2001. Reprinted by permission of Bayard Presse.

page 96: Ibrahim Issa. "Obama's Brother." Used by permission of the author.

Appendix E

page 124: *Apprendre le Québec*. http://www.immigration-quebec.gouv.qc.ca/publications/fr/divers/apprendrelequebec.pdf. Reprinted by permission of the Minister of Immigration and Cultural Communities, Québec, Canada.